MILLER'S
Classic Motorcycles
PRICE GUIDE

MILLER'S CLASSIC MOTORCYCLES PRICE GUIDE 1998/1999

Created and designed by
Miller's
The Cellars, High Street,
Tenterden, Kent, TN30 6BN
Tel: 01580 766411

Consultant: Judith Miller

General Editor: Mick Walker

Editorial and Production Co-ordinator: Sue Boyd
Editorial Assistants: Shirley Reeves, Jo Wood
Production Assistants: Gillian Charles, Nancy Charles
Advertising Executive: Jill Jackson
Advertising Assistant: Melinda Williams
Index compiled by: Hilary Bird
Design: Kari Reeves, Matthew Leppard, Shirley Reeves
Photographers: Ian Booth, Robin Saker, Nigel Clark

First published in Great Britain in 1997
by Miller's, an imprint of
Reed Consumer Books Limited,
Michelin House, 81 Fulham Road
London SW3 6RB
and Auckland, Melbourne, Singapore

© 1997 Reed Books Limited

A CIP catalogue record for this book is
available from the British Library

ISBN 1-84000-009-0

Illustrations and bromide output by A. S. Group, Ashford, Kent
Colour origination by Scantrans, Singapore
Printed and bound in England by William Clowes Ltd
Beccles and London

Miller's is a registered trademark of
Reed Books Ltd

Front cover illustrations:

The Practical Motor-Cyclist, by E. T. Brown. **£15–18**   *DM*
c1912 Triumph 3½hp. **£3,300–3,600**   *BKS*
1979 Suzuki TS250ER. **£1,000–1,200**   *PS*
Ducati Big 'D' Logo, 1950s. *PC*
Triumph brochure, 1920s. **£20–30**   *DM*
1948 Harley-Davidson WLC, 750cc. **£7,000–7,500**   *BLM*
1952 Gilera Saturno, 499cc. **£5,800–6,200**   *IVC*

MILLER'S
Classic Motorcycles
PRICE GUIDE

Consultant
Judith Miller

General Editor
Mick Walker

1998/9
Volume V

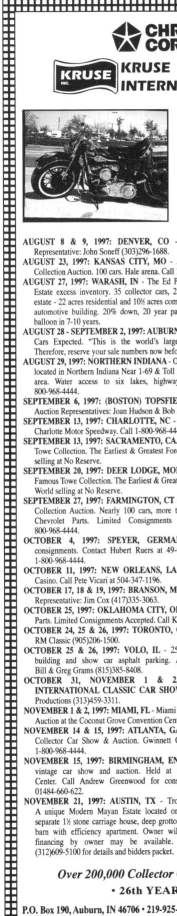

CONTENTS

ACKNOWLEDGEMENTS

The publishers would like to acknowledge the great assistance given by our consultants:

Malcolm Barber — Tel: 0171 228 8000

Rob Carrick — 5 Tinkers Lane, Wimbotsham, King's Lynn, Norfolk PE34 3QE Tel: 01366 388801

Stuart Donovan — Mayfair Motors, PO Box No 66, Lymington, Hants SO41 0XE

Stuart Mayhew — North Leicester Motorcycles Tel: 01530 263381

Brian Verrall — Woodlands, Mill Lane, Lower Beeding, Sussex RH13 6PX

We would like to extend our thanks to all auction houses, their press offices, and dealers who have assisted us in the production of this book, along with the organisers and press offices of the following events:

Coupes Moto Légende, Montlhéry
The International Classic Bike Show, Stafford
Louis Vuitton Classic
British Motorcycle Federation Rally

KEY TO ILLUSTRATIONS

*Each illustration and descriptive caption is accompanied by a letter code.
By referring to the following list of Auctioneers (denoted by *) and Dealers (·) the
source of any item may be immediately determined. Inclusion in this edition no way
constitutes or implies a contract or binding offer on the part of any of our
contributors to supply or sell the goods illustrated, or similar articles, at the prices
stated. Advertisers in this year's directory are denoted by † and Motorcycle Clubs by §.
If you require a valuation for an item, it is advisable to check whether the dealer or
specialist will carry out this service and if there is a charge. Please mention Miller's
when making an enquiry. Having found a specialist who will carry out your
valuation it is best to send a photograph and description of the item to the specialist
together with a stamped addressed envelope for the reply. A valuation by telephone is
not possible. Most dealers are only too happy to help you with your enquiry, however,
they are very busy people and consideration of the above points would be welcomed.*

ABCO § ABC Owners Club, D. A. Hales, The Hedgerows, Sutton St Nicholas, Hereford HR1 3BU Tel: 01432 880726

ABT · A. B. T. Engineering, 18 Hollis Gardens, Luckington, Chippenham, Wilts SN14 6NS Tel: 01666 840275

AC § Aermacchi Harley-Davidson Motor Club, Tuninfluiter 74, 3906, NS Veenendaal, The Netherlands

AMOC § AJS & Matchless Owners Club, Northants Classic Bike Centre, 25 Victoria Street, Irthlingborough, Northants NN9 5RG Tel: 01933 652155

ARD § Aircooled RD Club, Susan Gregory (Membership Secretary), 6 Baldwin Road, Burnage, Greater Manchester M19 1LY Tel: 0161 286 7539

AT · Andrew Tiernan Vintage & Classic Motorcycles, Old Railway Station, Station Road, Framlingham, Nr Woodbridge, Suffolk IP13 9EE Tel: 01728 724321

ATF A. T. Fletcher (Enthusiast & Collector), Lancashire

AtMC ·† Atlantic Motorcycles, 20 Station Road, Twyford, Berkshire RG10 9NT Tel: 01734 342266

BKS *† Brooks, Auctioneers & Valuers, 81 Westside, London SW4 9AY Tel: 0171 228 8000

BLM ·† Bill Little Motorcycles, Oak Farm, Braydon, Swindon, Wiltshire SN5 0AG Tel: 01666 860577

BMM Battlesbridge Motorcycle Museum, Muggeridge Farm, Maltings Road, Battlesbridge, Essex SS11 7RF Tel: 01268 769392/560866

BOC § BSA Owners Club, Rob Jones, 44 Froxfield Road, West Leigh, Havant, Hants PO9 5PW

BRIT * British Car Auctions Ltd, Classic & Historic Automobile Division, Auction Centre, Blackbushe Airport, Blackwater, Camberley, Surrey GU17 9LG Tel: 01252 878555

CARS · C.A.R.S. (Classic Automobilia & Regalia Specialists), 4-4a Chapel Terrace Mews, Kemp Town, Brighton, Sussex BN2 1HU Tel: 01273 601960

CCR ·† Charnwood Classic Restorations, 107 Central Road, Hugglescote, Coalville, Leicester LE67 2FL Tel: 01530 832357

COB · Cobwebs, 78 Northam Road, Southampton, Hampshire SO14 0PB Tel: 01703 227458

COEC § Cotton Owners & Enthusiasts Club, Stan White, 62 Cook Street, Avonmouth, Bristol, Dorset, BS11

CONQ · Conquest Motorcycles, 1 Victory Close Woolsbridge Industrial Estate, Three Legged Cross, Wimborne, Dorset BH21 6SX Tel: 01202 820009

COYS * Coys of Kensington, 2-4 Queens Gate Mews, London SW7 5QJ Tel: 0171 584 7444

CRC † Craven Collection of Classic Motorcycles, Brockfield Villa, Stockton-on-the-Forest, Yorks YO3 9UE Tel: 01904 488461/400493

CRMC § Classic Racing Motorcycle Club Ltd, Peter Haylock (Membership Secretary), 19 Kenilworth Avenue, Harold Farm, Romford, Essex RM3 9ME

CROW ·† Crowmarsh Classic Motorcycles, 34 Wantage Road, Didcot, Oxon OX11 0BT Tel: 01235 212727

CStC ·† Cake Street Classics, Bellview, Cake Street, Laxfield, Nr Woodbridge, Suffolk IP13 8EW Tel: 01986 798504

DM · Don Mitchell & Company, 132 Saffron Road, Wigston, Leicestershire LE18 4UP Tel: 0116 277 7669

DUC § Ducati Owners Club, Martin Littlebury, 32 Lawrence Moorings, Sawbridgeworth, Herts CM21 9PE

ELA * Eldreds Auctioneers & Valuers, 13-15 Ridge Park Road, Plympton, Plymouth, Devon PL7 2BS Tel: 01752 340066

FRC § Forgotten Racing Club, Mrs Chris Pinches, 73 High Street, Morton, Bourne, Lincolnshire PE10 0NR Tel: 01778 570535

GAZE * Thomas Wm Gaze & Son, 10 Market Hill, Diss, Norfolk IP22 3JZ Tel: 01379 651931

GB · George Beale Motorcycles, White Heather, New Road, Peggs Green, Coleorton, Leics LE67 8HL Tel: 01530 223611

GLC · Greenlooms Classics, Greenlooms Farm, Hargrave, Chester, CH3 7RX Tel: 01829 781636

GPT · Grand Prix Top Gear, The Old Mill, Mill End, Standon, Hertfordshire SG11 1LR Tel: 01279 843999

GRA § Greeves Riders Association, Dave & Brenda McGregor, 4 Longshaw Close, North Wingfield, Chesterfield, Staffs S42 5QR Tel: 01246 853846

HDM § Harley Davidson Manufacturers Club Tel: 01280 700101

HOLL * Dreweatt Neate Holloways, 49 Parsons Street, Banbury, Oxfordshire OX16 8PF Tel: 01295 253197

IMC § Indian Motorcycle Club, c/o John Chatterton (Membership Secretary), 183 Buxton Road, Newtown, Disley, Stockport, Cheshire SK12 3RA Tel: 01663 747106 (after 6pm)

IMO § Italian Motorcycle Owners Club, John Riches (Membership Secretary), 12 Wappenham Road, Abthorpe, Towcester, Northants NN12 8QU

JCZ § Jawa-CZ Owners Club, John Blackburn, 39 Bignor Road, Sheffield, Yorks S6 IJD

JUN • Junktion, The Old Railway Station, New Bolingbroke, Boston, Lincolnshire PE22 7LB Tel: 01205 480068

KAY • Kay Engineering Automotive Engineers, 26 Lichfield Road Sandhills, Nr Walsall, Staffordshire WS9 9PE Tel: 01543 377871

LE • Laurence Edscer, The Old House, The Square, Tisbury, Wilts SP3 6JP Tel: 01747 871200

LEV § LE Velo Club Ltd, Kevin Parsons, Chapel Mead, Blandford Hill, Winterbourne, Whitechurch, Blandford, Dorset DT11 0AB

LF * Lambert & Foster, 77 Commercial Road, Paddock Wood, Kent TN12 6DR Tel: 01892 832325

M * Morphets of Harrogate, 6 Albert Street, Harrogate, Yorks HG1 1JL Tel: 01423 530030

MAY •† Mayfair Motors, PO Box 66, Lymington, Hampshire SO41 0XE Tel: 01590 644476

MOC § Maico Owners Club, c/o Phil Hingston, 'No Elms', Goosey, Faringdon, Oxfordshire SN7 8PA Tel: 01367 710408

MoG § Moto Guzzi Club GB, Andy Harris (Membership Secretary), 158 Vale Road, Windsor, Berkshire SL4 5JN

MORI § Morini Riders Club, c/o Kevin Bennett, 1 Glebe Farm Cottages, Sutton Veney, Warminster, Wiltshire BA12 7AS Tel: 01985 840055

MSR § Marston Sunbeam Register, IMI Marston Ltd, Wobaston Road, Fordhouses, Wolverhampton, West Midlands WV10 6QJ

MVT § Military Vehicle Trust, PO Box 6, Fleet, Hampshire GU13 9PE

NAC § National Autocycle & Cyclemotor Club, 92 Waveney Road, Ipswich, Suffolk IP1 5DG

NDB § North Devon British Motorcycle Owners Club, 47 Old Town, Bideford, Devon EX39 3BH Tel: 01237 472237

NLM •† North Leicester Motorcycles, Whitehill Road, Ellistown, Leicestershire LE67 1EL Tel: 01530 263381

NOC § Norton Owners Club, c/o Dave Fenner, Beeches, Durley Brook Road, Durley, Southhampton, Hampshire SO32 2AR

NOC(C)§ Norton Owners Club (Cambridge Branch), William Riches (Secretary), 8 Coombelands Road, Royston, Hertfordshire SG8 7DW Tel: 01763 245131

OxM • Oxney Motorcycles, Rolvenden, Cranbrook, Kent TN17 4NP Tel: 01797 270119

PC Private Collection.

PM •† Pollard's Motorcycles, The Garage, Clarence Street, Dinnington, Sheffield, Yorkshire S31 7NA Tel: 01909 563310

PS *† Palmer Snell, 65 Cheap Street, Sherbourne, Dorset DT9 3BA Tel: 01935 812218

RAR * Romsey Auction Rooms, 86 The Hundred, Romsey, Hampshire SO51 8BX Tel: 01794 513331

ROW § Rotary Owners' Club, c/o David Cameron, Dunbar, Ingatestone Road, Highwood, Chelmsford, Essex CM1 3QU

RRM • RR Motor Services Ltd, Bethersden, Ashford, Kent TN26 3DN Tel: 01233 820219

RRN § Rolls Royce & NEI Vintage & Classic Motorcycle Section

RSS § Raleigh Safety Seven and Early Reliant Owners Club, Mike Sleap, 17 Courtland Avenue, Chingford, London E4 6DU

S * Sotheby's, 34-35 New Bond Street, London W1A 2AA Tel: 0171 493 8080

SW • Spinning Wheel Garage, Sheffield Road, Sheepbridge, Chesterfield, Derbys S41 9EH Tel: 01246 451772

TDC § Tamworth & District Classic Motorcycle Club Tel: Tamworth 281244

TRI § Trident and Rocket 3 Owners Club, PO Box 159, Cobham, Surrey KT11 2YG

Velo § Velocette Owners Club, Vic Blackman (Secretary), 1 Mayfair, Tilehurst, Reading, Berkshire RG3 4RA

VER •† Brian R. Verrall, Woodlands, Mill Lane, Lower Beeding, Sussex RH13 6PX Tel: 01403 891892

VIN • Vintage & Sports Car Garage Ltd, 47 West Street, Harrietsham, Kent ME17 1HX Tel: 01622 859570

VMC(P)§ Vintage Motor Cycle Club (Peterborough Branch), Jeremy Boycott Thurston (Secretary), 34 Heath Road, Helpston, Peterborough, Cambs PE6 7EG

VMSC § Vintage Motor Scooter Club, c/o Ian Harrop, 11 Ivanhoe Avenue, Lowton St Lukes, Nr Warrington, Cheshire WA3 2HX

WEED • Weeden Classic Restorations, Unit 5 Atlas Court, Hermitage Ind Est, Coalville, Leicestershire LE67 3FL Tel: 01530 811118

CLASSIC MOTORCYCLE RACING
How to get started

Most of us have watched in awe at the angle of lean achieved by the professional superstars at a national motorcycle race meeting, but at a Clubman's meeting the overall perspective changes. The grid is filled with enthusiastic amateur riders who are out there to enjoy themselves and it is at these meetings that some spectators may begin to think they are just as capable, if not better, than the riders on the track. At this point many spectators decide to make the transition to classic racing rider, but wonder how to get started.

The best way to enter the world of classic motorcycle racing is to join a club, such as the CRMC (Classic Racing Motorcycle Club), which caters for the rider who has a classic-eligible machine. The bike must have been manufactured before 1972 (1967 if it is a 2-stroke) and be fitted with period goodies only – no cast alloy wheels, oversized tyres or remote reservoir shock absorbers. Modern technology may be used, but only if hidden from view – this allows the use of belt drive primary transmissions and modern high-speed engine internals. A photograph and a brief description must be submitted before the eligibility committee of the CRMC. If the machine is not passed the reasons will be given and advice offered to help rectify infringements. Once accepted the bike will be issued with an eligibility certificate, which also carries its photograph to prevent any further modifications.

The type of racing class entered will depend on the rider's skills and finances. The CRMC cater for every size engine and this is further sub-divided into three groups: Group 1 races are for the thoroughbred TT, GP and Short Circuit machines; Group 2 races are for roadster-based and racing specials; with Group 3 races for production road and sports machines. As a genuine Group 1 racer now costs a king's ransom, many riders look towards Group 2 as the financial outlay is much less.

The 200cc class is a good starting point as it caters for the racing Tiger Cubs, Bantams, Villiers Specials and the Honda 175 Twin, but recently a few fast 50cc machines have turned up to put the frighteners on the class. The 250cc class has been split into singles and twins. The singles class is dominated by the Ducati, with a smattering of Greeves Silverstones, Cotton Telstars, Aermacchi and Royal Enfield machines. In the twins class the Suzuki Super Six is king and is usually followed home by the Yamaha, Ariel and Honda roadster-based racers. The 350cc class is also split into singles and twins, with the Ducati and Aermacchi singles fighting it out with the traditional British AJS, BSA and Norton racers; the twins race is totally dominated by the Honda K4. In the larger capacity classes British racing motorcycles hail supreme, be it a single, twin or a 3 cylinder machine, as 4 cylinder bikes are barred to keep out the early Japanese fours. Below are listed the annual 'CMRC championship classes' that riders can qualify for.

Honda UK	200cc
Arai Helmets	250cc singles
Honda UK	250cc twins
Barber Frames	350cc singles
Summerfield Eng	350cc Group 1 singles
Honda UK	350 cc twins
Summerfield Eng	500 cc Group 1 singles
Reynold Chain	500 cc Group 2
Carol Nash	750 cc
Boyer Bransden	Unlimited
Carol Nash	Group 3 Production
NJB Shocks	Post Classic
Atlantic M/C	Sidecars

To ease entry into the classic racing scene the CRMC hold classic parades at all their meetings. Machines of all sizes and types parade together – newcomers on shoestring specials and old timers on priceless racers.

The transition from parades to class racing requires an ACU (Auto Cycle Union) licence. To obtain this licence an application for a novice licence must be countersigned by the club under whose rules the rider will be racing, together with a medical examination report on the rider. This licence will entitle the holder to race as a novice wearing an orange jacket. The novice jacket can only be discarded once the rider has completed ten meetings to the satisfaction of the Clerk of the Course. These ten events must take place at over three different venues.

Once the rider fulfils all novice requirements they will be given a 'restricted road racing licence', which entitles entry into restricted club events. From here the rider can then go for a national licence, which requires further signatures. This licence entitles the holder to enter national events, but here the competition gets very fierce.

One ritual to which all riders are subjected at every meeting – be it parading or racing – is that of scrutineering, where both the rider and the machine are checked for compliance with club rules and the ACU code of safety. The riders' racing suit, gloves, boots and helmet are all checked to ensure they meet current safety requirements and standards.

Throughout the summer season the CRMC organises a series of events at various venues, with the race of the year at Snetterton, Norfolk, in late September. These meetings are always well attended, professionally run and enjoyed by the riders from all parts of the UK and the Continent.

For further details on how to join the CRMC and a list of racing events write to the CRMC membership secretary, Peter Haycock, 19 Kenilworth Avenue, Harold Park, Romford, Essex EM3 9NE

Rob Carrick

HOW TO USE THIS BOOK

It is our aim to make this guide easy to use. Motorcycle marques are listed alphabetically and then chronologically. Autocycles, Dirt Bikes, Military Motorcycles, Monkey Bikes, Mopeds, Racing Bikes, Forgotten Era Racing, Scooters, Sidecars and Specials are located after the marques, towards the end of the book. In the Memorabilia section objects are grouped by type. If you cannot find what you are looking for please consult the index which starts on page 174.

Marque Introduction
provides an overview of the marque including factory changes and in some instances the history of a particular model. Introductions change from year to year and not every section will begin with an introduction.

DOUGLAS 37

DOUGLAS (British 1906–57)
The Bristol-based Douglas Foundry took up motorcycle production in 1907 with a machine powered by a horizontally-opposed twin, and the company would kept faith with this engine layout until it ceased motorcycle production in 1957. Fore-and-aft installation made for a slim machine with a low centre of gravity, and the design's virtues were soon demonstrated in competition, Douglas machines taking first, second and fourth places in the 1912 Junior TT in the Isle of Man. Douglas were quick to realise the advantages of the countershaft gearbox, its 3-speed entries gaining the Team Prize in the 1914 Six Days Trial, a conspicuous success which resulted in the firm obtaining a wartime contract for the supply of military machines.

1914 Douglas 2¾hp, 348cc, fore-and-aft horizontally opposed twin cylinder engine, belt final drive.
£5,500–6,000 *BLM*

1912 Douglas Flat Twin 2¾hp, 348cc.
£6,500–7,000 *BKS*

r. **1919 Douglas 2¾hp Model V,** 348cc.
£4,600–5,000 *BKS*

Described in contemporary advertising as 'the business man's ideal mount possessed of that ease of control and turn of speed which is the making of a perfect touring machine'. The Douglas 2¾hp had, of course, been well proven in military service in WWI, its 348cc engine proving durable in adverse conditions and in the hands of novice riders.

1924 Douglas T5, 348cc.
£3,500–4,000 *BKS*

r. **1957 Douglas Dragonfly,** 348cc.
£2,600–3,000 *BKS*

The Dragonfly arrived in 1955 and featured a revised engine with stronger crank case, single carburettor, and updated electrics and ignition. The duplex frame employed a conventional swinging arm with Girling dampers in place of the preceding torsion bar arrangement, while the Radiadraulic front fork gave way to an Earles-type leading link set-up.

Caption
provides a brief description of the motorcycle or item, and could include comments on its history, mileage, any restoration work carried out and current condition.

Source Code
refers to the 'Key to Illustrations' on page 7 which lists the details of where the item was photographed, and whether it is from a dealer, club or auction house. Advertisers are also indicated on this page.

Price Guide
price ranges are worked out by a team of trade and auction house experts, and are based on actual prices realised. Remember that Miller's is a PRICE GUIDE not a PRICE LIST and prices are affected by many variables such as location, condition, desirability and so on. Don't forget that if you are selling it is quite likely you will be offered less than the price range. Price ranges for items sold at auction include the buyer's premium.

Italicised Footnote
covers relevant additional information about a motorcycle's restoration and/or racing history, designer, racing drivers and special events in which it may have participated.

FOREWORD

*M*iller's Classic Motorcycles Price Guide is now in its fifth
year and I am pleased once again to provide the Foreword.
There is, perhaps no better guide to the growth of interest
in classic and vintage motorcycles than the enthusiastic support
worldwide events catering for these machines are attracting.

Over the past five years I have seen attendance at the Goodwood
Festival of Speed, possibly the best supported and most prestigious
event of its kind, grow from five figures to 100,000. Wearing two
hats as I do on these occasions, with my career spanning both two
and four wheels, it is intriguing and satisfying to see the
enthusiasts; the young, not so young and many families, gazing in
awe over a 1956 MV Agusta 4 cylinder Grand Prix machine or a
Manx Norton.

The thrill associated with motorcycles at Goodwood and again in
New Zealand, where I rode my 1939 Georg Meier supercharged
BMW Kompressor, together with the tremendous support I
received when I attended events in Montlhèry in France and
Vallelunga in Italy this year, brought home to me the ever
increasing interest in machines that are part of motorcycling
heritage and the part that the younger generation is now playing
in keeping the classic movement so alive and well.

Prices obtained in both private sales and in the auction houses
would appear to have steadily improved, although thankfully
buyers have, I believe, become more selective and better informed.
The marketplace can, however, be a perilous place and should you
make a mistake with a classic motorcycle it can be costly to rectify.
Time spent on research and gaining knowledge pays dividends.
Miller's Classic Motorcycles Price Guide is an essential reference
book for both enthusiast and professional motorcycle owner alike
to help with this task. With numerous illustrations ranging from
ABC to Yamaha you are sure to find what you are looking for.

THE MOTORCYCLE MARKET

The international market for classic and collectors' motorcycles is distinctly different in character to that of the classic car market – as it always has been. It is far more enthusiast-driven, less trendy and, therefore, less susceptible to the whims and dictates of fashion and the economy, except in respect of the highest priced and more desirable machines. The sector which shows the largest growth is in the more recent period from the 1950s onwards.

Two factors have encouraged this. First the Vintage Motor Cycle Club (and most other clubs for older machines) operates a 25 year 'rolling date' for eligibility. This means that every year another batch of machines becomes 'of age' and achieves classic status. The second factor, which has tended to underline the first, is the DVLA's concession of exemption from VED for machines over 25 years old, which has encouraged greater use of machines already in preservation, and has discouraged the scrapping of machines approaching the age demarcation line. Since enthusiasts tend to identify with machines with which they grew up, and since generally the 'newer' classics are cheaper (if unrestored) than very old ones, not only is the supply of classics maintained but so is each new generation of enthusiasts.

Although the 1990s have seen a steady improvement in prices generally, price increases have not been dramatic in any other than the top echelon bikes. What has been more noticeable is that the market has grown and more bikes are now selling, although the number of annual sales has remained about the same. Inevitably this means that existing sales have become larger, as evidenced by Brooks' sale at the International Classic Bike Show at Stafford in April, where almost 450 lots of motorcycles and related material came under the hammer. It is significant that at this well-attended event interest remained strong throughout the sale, with machines finding new homes right up to the last lot. Stafford tends to be looked upon as the barometer for the whole classic bike market, and with sales totalling over £500,000 at this event alone, it may be seen to be extremely healthy.

Last year Brooks sold over £1 million worth of motorcycles, and the fact that they achieved half of that total at their first sale of the year is a good indication of current trends. Past experience has, however, dictated the nature of bikes currently on offer. With the market apparently saturated with Japanese relatively late high-performance competition machines with high prices, these have largely disappeared from sales, and their owners are doubtless waiting for a more opportune time at which to re-offer them.

Vincents and Brough-Superiors appear to be achieving prices commensurate with those which we previously saw in the heady days of the late 1980s, with two Series 'C' Vincent Black Shadows making aggregate prices of £14,375 and £12,765 at auction, and a 1936 Brough-Superior side valve SS80 making £10,350. British competition bikes of an earlier era are also doing well, with examples of Rudge Ulster Grand Prix, Excelsior Manxman and AJS 7R and K10 making £8,050, £8,050, £8,050 and £5,060 respectively at auction.

Dealers have also been actively buying and selling at auction, with retail sales improving although foreign buyers may be more selective on their buying trips to the UK with the ever-strengthening pound. However, the pound's strength against Continental currencies means that UK buyers can buy profitably abroad even allowing for import taxes and the tide of motorcycles ebbs and flows accordingly. Dealers stock would appear to be good with the emphasis on quality rather than quantity. Advertising by the trade is prolific in the specialist magazines indicating a continuing buoyancy in the marketplace.

Machines which consistently fail to excite interest include most Soviet types, Japanese non-sporting lightweights, and unrestored 'grey porridge' where the resulting machine simply doesn't justify the time and expense of restoration. Lightweight 2-stroke flat-tankers of the 1920s are still very affordable, and the same goes for most machines that are impractical for anything other than specialised events. Buyers for Nortons, especially Manx and International models are selective; proven history and matching frame and engine numbers being important. Good vintage Sunbeams, particularly sporting models, continue to find buyers, especially in Germany.

While sales of classic cars have proliferated recently, there appears to have been a polarisation of available business in the two-wheeled world to just three auction houses, with Brooks holding four sales purely devoted to bikes each year, Sotheby's continuing to sell bikes but combining them as an adjunct to their car sales, and Palmer Snell who hold two auction events at Shepton Mallett each year.

On a broader note the abolition of EU trade barriers in 1993 has done much to encourage European buyers to both buy and sell in the UK and along with the abandonment of Customs controls and VAT at internal EU borders trade in classic motorcycles is increasing. The more bidders from the Continent make their presence known in British salesrooms, the stronger becomes the home market particularly among private buyers determined to prevent machines going abroad, and the bolder dealers become when safe in the knowledge that they can sell their classic motorcycles overseas, as well as to UK buyers. The future continues to look bright for classic motorcycles.

Malcolm Barber

ABC *(British 1913–22)*

The first ABC in-line flat twin appeared in 1913. Of these early models (built 1913–17) only three or four exist today. From 1919 onwards the ABC twin was made under licence by the Sopwith Aviation & Engineering Co in Kingston-upon-Thames. It had a duplex frame with leaf spring suspension, in-unit flat twin engine set across the frame with clutch, gearbox all bevel drive. Some 2,200 were made, of which about 10 per cent survive,

a remarkably high number for a vintage motorcycle. Various types of valve gear conversion sets were made available later, and speedometers, electric lighting sets and sidecar outfits were optional extras. From 1920 to 1924 the machine was also made under licence in France by Gnome et Rhone. Some 3,000 French models were manufactured, but relatively few seem to have survived. There is a British-based owners' club.

1921 ABC Twin Cylinder, 398cc.
£4,250–5,000 *VER*

AERMACCHI *(Italian 1950–78)*

l. **1954 Aermacchi 125U,** 123cc, 2-stroke, horizontal cylinder, leading link front forks.
£1,200–1,250 *AC*

r. **1962 Aermacchi Ala Verde,** 246cc overhead valve, unit construction, 4-speed, wet clutch.
£1,600–1,900 *PC*

AJS *(British 1909–66)*

AJS, together with Matchless, became more commonly known as AMC (Associated Motor Cycles). Matchless and AJS had joined forces when the latter hit the financial rocks in mid-1931, after over extending themselves just prior to the Wall Street crash of October 1929. This meant that the AJS empire Stevens brothers (Harry, George, Jack and Joe) was effectively taken over by the rival Matchless concern. This entailed a move from the original Wolverhampton base to the Matchless headquarters in Plumstead Road, Woolwich, London.

Although Matchless and AJS were always the hub of AMC, the grouping became ever larger, beginning in 1938 with the acquisition of Sunbeam (which was subsequently sold on to BSA in 1943). Next came Francis Barnett (1947), James (1952), Brockhouse (1959) and, also in 1952, the big daddy of them all, Norton. The latter operation did not, however, move to Plumstead from its original home in Bracebridge Street, Birmingham, until 1963. By then the rot had already begun to set in.

This was caused by a combination of things: badge engineering rather than new models, and a whole series of lightweight models that did not match what the public wanted – examples being the AJS/Matchless 250/350 'Lightweight' unit construction singles, the Norton Jubilee, Navigator and Electra twins, and the simply awful AMC-designed 2-stroke engine which the company hoped would replace the bought-in Villiers units which James and Francis Barnett used.

The death in 1954 of Charlie Collier, the 70 year-old co-founder of Matchless did not help matters. Even though the AMC group left the 1950s in profit, the writing was by now clearly on the wall, with its big singles and twins, although still selling well, in urgent need of updating (for example both BSA and Triumph unveiled more modern unit construction twins in the 1960s).

After years of profit AMC suddenly lost a quarter of a million pounds in 1960. It was even worse the following year. And although an attempt was made to jazz up its ageing model line, it was to no avail and the downward slide continued – at an even greater pace.

The final straw came when AJS and Matchless models began to sprout Norton wheels and forks. The buyers of the two former marques rightly argued that if they wanted a Norton they would buy one – not an 'Ajay' or 'Matchbox'.

Of course, this state of affairs could not continue for long, and on 4 August 1966 it was announced that the directors had asked the company's bankers to appoint a receiver. It was the end of an era.

1928 AJS 350 Big Port, 348cc, single cylinder, acetylene lighting.
£5,000–6,000 *CONQ*
Superb, original example of this classic 'Ajay'.

1912 AJS 350, 349cc, single cylinder inlet over exhaust engine, 2-speed, chain final drive.
£5,000–5,500 *VER*

1927 AJS 500 Big Port, 498cc.
£5,250–5,750 *PM*

1953 AJS Model 18S, 497cc, 'jampot' rear shocks, alloy cylinder head, magneto ignition, fully restored, excellent condition.
£3,500–4,000 *WEED*

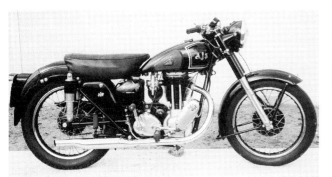

1953 AJS Model 18S, 497cc, 'jampot' rear units.
£2,500–2,700 *BLM*

1954 AJS Model 16MS, 348cc.
£1,300–1,500 *BKS*

Epitomising the traditional concept of the British heavyweight single, AMC's post-war 350cc and 500cc models combined an excellent standard of finish with tried and tested mechanics. From 1948 on, the option of front and rear springing with hydraulic damping was available.

l. **1954 AJS Model 20 Springer Twin,** 498cc, overhead valve twin, swinging arm rear suspension, 'jampot' shocks, full width front hub, completely restored.
£1,900–2,300 *PC*

1955 AJS Model 18S, 497cc.
£3,000–3,400 *BLM*

1959 AJS Model 18S, 497cc, AMC gearbox, improved alloy primary chain case, original specification.
£2,200–2,600 *BLM*

1959 AJS Model 31 De Luxe, 646cc, overhead valve, twin cylinder, AMC gearbox.
£2,600–2,900 *BLM*

1962 AJS Model 31, 646cc, touring version of AMC's pushrod twin, non-standard seat.
£2,500–2,700 *BLM*

1962 AJS Model 8 Lightweight, 348cc, composite frame, steel stampings, tubular construction.
£900–1,200 *BLM*

These unit singles were never as popular as the earlier pre-unit models.

1978 AJS Stormer, 247cc, alloy petrol tank, nickel-plated frame, alloy wheel rims, plastic mudguards, 'enduro' trim, full lighting set, 1,600 miles recorded from new, excellent condition.
£1,400–1,600 *BKS*

ARIEL *(British 1902–70)*
The Square Four

It was extremely unfortunate that Ariel's most prestigious and technically interesting design was born in a world in the grip of the worst depression in history. As a consequence sales never reached anything like the potential demanded.

At a time when the term 'superbike' had yet to be coined, the Square Four was one of the few motorcycles of its era that really deserved the title (others would have included the Brough-Superior SS100 and the ill-fated Matchless Silver Hawk).

The first Square Four was revealed to the public at the London Motorcycle Show in November 1930. It was a 500cc model with overhead camshaft operation of its valves and cost just over £75. First deliveries began in March 1931, and during that year a total of 957 units were sold. Then, at the 1931 London Show, a 600cc model made its debut. Although the original smaller engined device was still available only 45 were subsequently sold and it was soon axed, whereas in 1932 the new 600cc Square Ariel sold a total of 1,174 machines.

Between 1932 and 1936 only the 600 overhead camshaft version was available and some 5,000 examples left the Ariel works. In 1937 a new and considerably different 1000 (997cc) model with pushrod operated valves went on sale, but only 379 were actually built (against 1,048 of the 600 variant).

Sales continued in small numbers up to September 1939, and with the Square Four being adjudged unsuitable for the Forces (although a few machines went to the police and civil defence authorities) production of any significance did not resume until after the end of the conflict.

In 1949 the engine was redesigned with a light alloy block and head and was referred to as the MkI. In 1953, the MkII or 'four pipe' model was introduced, which featured detachable light alloy exhaust manifolds on each side with two header pipes neatly Siamesed into single pipes and silencers. Less than 4,000 MkIIs were built, and production came to a halt in 1959 when the last MkIIG model left the Birmingham Selly Oak factory.

1947 Ariel NH Red Hunter, 346cc.
£3,000–3,300 *BKS*

l. **1927 Ariel Model E,** 500cc, girder forks, hand gear change, twin port engine.
£3,000–3,500 *PC*

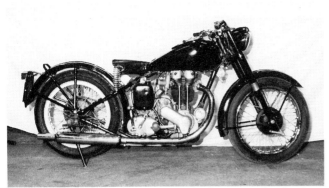

1953 Ariel Square Four MkII, 998cc, restored, very good condition.
£3,000–3,300 *BKS*

Introduced in 1953, the 'four pipe' MkII with re-designed cylinder head was a genuine 100mph machine. With its limitless reserves of pulling power and innate smoothness, the model was always a favourite of the sidecar brigade.

1948 Ariel VH Red Hunter, 497cc, single port overhead valve single cylinder, rigid frame, non-standard alloy rear wheel rim.
£1,400–1,600 *PS*

l. **1953 Ariel KH 500 Overhead Valve Twin,** 499cc.
£2,500–2,800 *BKS*

Much of Ariel's wartime work was on projects other than the manufacture of motorcycles although the 350 W/NG was produced by them throughout. Post-war Val Page designed a 500cc vertical twin. The new twin was designated the KH and enabled the factory to announce a full range of singles, twins and fours which was in the 1950s impressive for a British manufacturer.

1956 Ariel Square Four MkII, 998cc.
£4,500–5,000 *BKS*

Designed by Edward Turner, the Square Four was first shown at Olympia in 1930. Originally an overhead camshaft 500, the model grew to 601cc before a total redesign saw it emerge as the Model 4G, with 995cc overhead valve engine, in 1937. Anstey-link plunger rear suspension became an option in 1939, but was not offered again until 1946, when a telescopic front fork replaced the previous girder type. An exercise in weight shedding saw the cast iron cylinder head and barrel replaced by alloy components for 1949, the revised model, now capable of 90mph-plus, being known as the MkI. Introduced in 1953, the 'four pipe' MkII with redesigned cylinder head was a genuine 100mph machine. Square Four production, along with that of all other Ariel 4 strokes, ceased in 1959.

1956 Ariel NH Red Hunter, 346cc, 18bhp at 5600rpm, headlamp cowl, off-white dual seat, full width hubs.
£1,000–1,200 *PM*

This was the last of the famous NH Red Hunters.

r. **1958 Ariel 4G Square Four MkII,** 998cc, stored for 20 years, requires attention, engine in running order, wheels rebuilt, new exhaust system, cycle parts, gearbox and paintwork good.
£2,800–3,000 *BKS*

l. **1962 Ariel Leader,** 247cc, air-cooled, 2-stroke, twin cylinder with unit gearbox, fully restored, excellent condition.
£2,000–2,200 *BKS*

Designed by Val Page and his team, and launched in 1958, the Leader broke with British tradition in its frame and suspension design, employing a stiff, fabricated-steel beam instead of tubes, and a trailing link front fork. Another unusual feature was the fuel tank's location within the frame – what appeared to be a conventional tank was in fact a storage compartment. Detachable panels enclosing the engine and most of the rear wheel extended forwards to meet legshields and screen, and the rear chain was fully enclosed. Although a highly promising design capable of further development, it was axed by BSA in 1965.

> **Don't Forget!**
> *If in doubt please refer to the 'How to Use' section at the beginning of this book.*

r. **1964 Ariel Arrow,** 247cc, air-cooled, 2-stroke, twin cylinder, with inclined cylinders, iron barrels, alloy heads.
£600–800 *PC*

This was the final year for the basic Arrow, although the Leader, Super Sports (Golden Arrow) and 200 Arrow all soldiered on into 1965.

BEARDMORE-PRECISION
(British 1921–24)

1923 Beardmore-Precision 350 Side Valve, 349cc, 3-speed Sturmey-Archer gearbox, final drive by chain, good condition.
£3,100–3,400 *BKS*

BENELLI *(Italian 1911–)*

1936 Benelli 250 Sport, 247cc, overhead camshaft single cylinder, 67 x 70mm bore and stroke, ignition by contact breakers, maximum speed 70mph.
£3,300–4,000 *PC*

Note the deeply finned sump and dynamo at the front of the crank case.

l. **1979 Benelli 2C Electronica,** 231cc, restored, excellent condition.
£775–850 *BKS*

In 1975 a brace of 2C Benelli 250cc 2-stroke machines were entered in the Isle of Man Production TT. The machines were fitted with standard engines and only the cycle parts were altered to suit the racing conditions. This was an effort made by the UK concessionaires who were aware that in Italy these engines tuned and fed by Mukuni carburettors were producing speeds of 120mph. UK sales were boosted by the entry of these 2 machines, but the competition from the Japanese market was nevertheless too strong for them to make a direct impression.

BIANCHI *(Italian 1897–1967)*

One man alone dominated the pioneering days of the embryonic Italian motorcycle at the turn of the century – Edoardo Bianchi. Born on 17 July 1865, Bianchi was brought up in a Milanese orphanage, but from an early age showed a remarkable aptitude for engineering. In 1885, at the age of 20, he set up a small machine shop for bicycle manufacture. Bianchi moved to larger premises in 1888, where he produced the first Italian vehicle (a bicycle) with pneumatic tyres. The business expanded at a great pace throughout the 1890s when cycling became as fashionable in Italy as elsewhere in Europe.

In 1897, Edoardo Bianchi carried out tests with a De Dion single cylinder engine mounted in a tricycle. Although the prototype caught fire there was still great satisfaction of having been the first Italian to propel a vehicle without resorting to muscle power. By the turn of the century Bianchi was not only selling tricycles with the 269cc De Dion engine mounted behind the rear axle, but was already planning the next stage which included motorcycles and cars.

In 1901 the first prototype motorcycle appeared, going on sale the following year. The production version was the first Bianchi vehicle to be constructed entirely out of components manufactured within its Milanese factory, including a 2hp engine built under licence from De Dion.

In 1905, by which time it was also producing automobiles, the company was incorporated as Edoardo Bianchi & Co. From then until the end of WWI, Bianchi's turnover increased quite dramatically year on year. The developments had been greatly assisted by the opening of a vast new plant in 1902 in Via Nino Bixio, Milan. This allowed not only expansion but also the development of improved models, including a single with such luxuries as magneto ignition, leading link front forks and belt drive. In 1905 a new design of Truffault forks appeared, and by 1910 a brand new 500 made Bianchi the envy of every other motorcycle manufacturer in Italy. It was the great success of his brilliantly conceived 498cc model that really put Bianchi on the road to success.

During the war Bianchi concentrated on aero engines but also supplied a 649cc V-twin engine and a purpose-built C75 military model. These were manufactured in considerable numbers. At the end of the hostilities the V-twin was increased in size to 741cc.

As the factory was about to enter the 1920s, a period of even greater expansion beckoned, with not only speed and racing records broken by Bianchi machinery but also the first real push for international sales. Famous not only for motorcycles, but cars and pedal cycles as well, the famous Bianchi name only survives today as manufacturers of bicycles – albeit as part of the massive Piaggio empire. But even so, Italian motorcycling (and motoring) history owes much to the genius that was Edoardo Bianchi.

1951 Bianchi 125 Turismo, 124cc, piston port 2-stroke, 4-speed, telescopic forks, swing arm rear suspension.
£900–950 *PC*

This is one of the first of the post-war Bianchi models.

1961 Bianchi Bernina, 124cc, overhead valve single cylinder, 4 speed gearbox, unit construction, wet sump, full width alloy brake hubs.
£1,100–1,300 *PC*

l. **1960 Bianchi Tonale,** 174cc, overhead camshaft single cylinder, battery/coil 6 volt electrics, bore and stroke 60 x 61.8mm, 8.3bhp at 6000rpm.
£1,800–2,000 *IMO*

This was Bianchi's top selling roadster of the late 1950s and early '60s.

1964 Bianchi 350 Twin Racer, 348cc.
£30,000–35,000 *PC*

This example was raced in the 1960s by factory rider, Remo Venturi, with considerable success. Specification includes 65 x 52.5mm bore and stroke, 6-speed gearbox and large drum brakes. There were also 422cc and 498cc versions for use in the 500cc class. Some 7 or 8 examples in total were constructed and today only 2 or 3 survive.

1963 Bianchi Tonale, 174cc.
£1,600–1,800 *CRMC*

This particular Tonale has been converted for classic racing events. Changes include Yamaha brakes, rear sets, clip-ons, megaphone exhaust, tachometer, racing tank and seat, plus tuned motor.

BIMOTA *(Italian 1973–)*

The Bimota marque was born more by accident than design, though for superbike enthusiasts the accident was a singularly happy event. Massimo Tamburini owned a heating business in the town of Rimini, on the Adriatic coast, an area of Italy which had long been a centre for both racing and motorcycle manufacture. As a hobby, Tamburini modified several local riders' machines to make them not only faster but also lighter and sharper to handle. His efforts were rewarded with success, and before very long his work on one particular machine, the MV Agusta 600 four, had gained the admiration of the entire Italian biking fraternity.

It was an event in the summer of 1972 which was the real key to the birth of Bimota: a routine test session at the Misano race circuit where Tamburini, his friend Giuseppe Morri and racer Luigi Anelli were testing a specially framed Honda CB750. A journalist who was present wrote a feature about Tamburini's Honda, creating such a wave of interest that a commercial organisation was established to meet the consequent influx of orders. The company took its name from the three partners who set it up – Bianchi, Morri and Tamburini.

The new venture began trading on 1 January 1973. In addition to the Honda, Tamburini had just completed a pure racing machine powered by a Yamaha TR2 2-stroke engine. This too was an instant success, and in 1975

Johnny Cecotto won the 350cc World Championship on a Bimota-framed TZ Yamaha.

The first real Bimota superbike was the Suzuki GS750-engined SB2 (the SB1 was a racer) which made its debut at the Bologna Show in January 1977. The next development in the evolution of the Bimota street bike came at the 1977 Milan Show in the shape of the KB1, housing either a Kawasaki 903 or 1015cc double overhead camshaft 4 cylinder motor.

The publicity and resultant sales success led to yet more mouthwatering superbikes, and soon Honda wanted a piece of the action as well, and later Yamaha – all with official support from the respective companies. During this period, Bimota introduced several innovations for production roadsters, including variable steering geometry, the space frame, and a standard of workmanship previously unseen.

During the late 1970s and early 1980s, the Company boomed. Then came the crunch, at the 1983 Milan Show Bimota was foolish enough to display a prototype of a totally new bike – the futuristic Tesi – which it didn't have ready for sale. The result was no sales and bankruptcy. The Compay was saved only by government support and the first ever Ducati powered product, the 1985 DB1. The success of this one motorcycle ensured a comeback which continues in the late 1990s with Ducati and Yamaha engines, plus Bimota's own water-cooled 500cc 2-stroke street bike.

1980 Bimota SB2/2, 944cc.
£6,900–7,400 *PC*

This model has basically a 1977 Suzuki GS750 engine with the standard 65mm bores increased to 73mm, giving 944cc, with Yoshimura cams, valve gear, pistons and 29mm carburettors.

1982 Bimota KB2, 553cc.
£3,900–4,200 *IMO*

The KB2 laser was introduced in 1981, and used the air-cooled GP550 Kawasaki engine. Maximum speed is 125mph.

BMW (German 1923–)

1960 BMW R60, 594cc.
£3,000–4,000 *BLM*

In 1955 BMW launched its new Earles fork range. Included in this line were the R50, R60 and R69. This particular machine has the twin sprung saddles, rather than the more usual Denfold dual seat. These R60s make fine sidecar machines.

1973 BMW R90 Special, 898cc.
£1,000–1,200 *BKS*

Miller's is a price GUIDE
not a price LIST

BOWN (British 1922–24)

l. **1951 Bown MC,** 99cc.
£350–400 *PS*

This name from the 1920s was revived in 1950 and used by the firm for its autocycle, which replaced the Aberdale they had built previously. The machine was revised to use the single speed Villiers 2F engine. For 1951 the autocycle was joined by a small motorcycle, powered by a Villiers IF engine with 2-speed gearbox. This employed a cradle frame with duplex downtubes and tubular forks.

BRADBURY (British 1901–25)

1913 Bradbury Side Valve, 554cc.
£4,500–5,000 *ELA*

In excellent original condition and with the same owner since 1950, complete with Sunbeam Pioneer Certificate, old type log book and V5 registration document.

BROUGH-SUPERIOR *(British 1919–39)*

Often referred to as 'the Rolls-Royce of motorcycles', the Brough-Superior was built from 1919 to 1939, and even though only 3,000 were built in total, they carved a special place in the hearts of motorcyclists the world over.

Based in Nottingham, George Brough benefited from the expertise of his father William, who had built his own cars and tricycles powered by De Dion engines at the turn of the century. While William favoured flat-twin engines, George immediately plumped for the V-twin and it was to be seen on the vast majority of his models.

Entering production in 1921, the first Brough-Superior was tested by *The Motor Cycle* on 20 January that year in both solo and sidecar trim. It was powered by a specially tuned 986cc overhead valve JAP engine with Sturmey Archer 3 speed gearbox, Brampton Biflex forks and Enfield cush-drive hub. Costing £175 in solo specification it had, for the time, a superb top gear performance which ranged from 8 to 80mph, while its appearance and quality were deemed to be truly excellent. The latter was helped by heavy nickel plating of many components. The oval bulbous plated tank, which was to be a standard Brough feature, was not only a focal point of interest but practical too.

George Brough was ably supported by his right-hand man Ike Webb, and together they created a line of machines which are still held in awe today. Probably the most famous of all was the SS100, a 50° V-twin introduced at the Olympia Show in November 1924. It was sold with a guarantee that it would exceed 100mph on the track. The design was based on the record-breaking exploits of Bert le Vack and featured a sturdy duplex cradle frame to which were fitted Castle forks, similar in principle to a Harley-Davidson design.

In 1932, a machine designed for sidecar work employed a 800cc Austin water-cooled 4 cylinder engine with the unusual feature of twin rear wheels and shaft drive. But the most unique of all Broughs was the Dream, a 997cc flat four-engined model which was displayed at Earl's Court in 1938 but never entered production due to the outbreak of war.

Celebrated riders aplenty rode Brough-Superiors, including such racing names as Bert le Vack, Eric Fernihough, E. C. E. Baragwanath, Freddie Dixon and Noel Pope. Besides their track successes, Fernihough and Pope were also notable speed record-breakers.

The Nottingham company's most famous customer was Colonel T. E. Lawrence (Lawrence of Arabia), who rode Brough-Superiors for over a decade and, it is sad to record, met his death while riding a Brough in 1935.

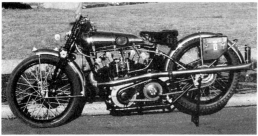

1927 Pendine Brough, 998cc.
£35,000–37,000 *PM*

Named after the famous record-breaking exploits achieved by a Brough at Pendine Sands, this machine has a proud history and is one of the most famous of all George Brough's models – only 20 examples being manufactured.

1936 Brough-Superior SS80, 986cc, Norton International gearbox, later seat and front mudguard, rebuilt, engine rebored.
£10,400–11,400 *BKS*

Writing of the new SS100 late in 1935, George Brough said 'I guarantee that the new SS100 is the fastest and – with the exception of the new SS80 – the quietest machine on the road bar none.' 1935 had been a glorious year for Brough-Superior with Eric Fernihough achieving fastest time in every event entered, first in every class entered and record for every course competed. These notable achievements boosted sales and Brough offered the SS100, SS80 and 11-50 models for the 1936 season. The side valve SS80 offered the best performance of any comparable side valve mount and this model, with Druid forks and rigid frame, was listed at £90 ex-works when supplied to Hooley's Garage in 1936.

r. **1938 Brough-Superior SS80,** 986cc, side valve V-twin engine, plunger rear suspension, chrome petrol tank, restored, very good condition, requires recommissioning.
£11,000–13,000 *S*

BSA *(British 1906–7, late 1970s–)*
Star Twins and The Maudes Trophy

During 1952, relatively unnoticed and unheralded, came one of the most remarkable performances ever by British motorcycles. At the end of August an ACU (Auto Cycle Union) official travelled to BSA's works at Small Heath, Birmingham, and selected three 500 A7 Star Twins at random from a batch of 37 on the production line. BSA decided to make an attempt to win the coveted Maudes Trophy, awarded by the ACU for the most meritorious reliability performance of the year. The object of the exercise was to subject these three standard machines to a lifetime of hard work within the space of a few short weeks. And since the ISDT (International Six Days Trial) was the ultimate test, the event was included on the itinerary!

Having been selected the machines were lightly modified – gearing, tyres, even mapholder etc – and then sealed and locked up until the test commenced in early September. A team of highly experienced riders were selected: Norman Vanhouse, Fred Rist and Brian Martin. They made their official start from the ACU's offices in London, crossed the channel to The Hague and then travelled via Antwerp, Paris, Geneva, Zurich and Innsbruck to Bad Ausee, where the ISDT was based that year.

From 17–23 September the trio were engaged in serious competition. In truly appalling conditions (which saw the official British teams decimated) the three BSAs went on to complete the event without trouble and penalty free – so good in fact that BSA was able to advertise that the three stock Star Twins were the only British team to finish with clean sheets!

Immediately following this arduous test the three riders set off on the return journey via Stuttgart, Düsseldorf, Hanover, Hamburg, Kiel, Copenhagen, then ferry to Malmö in Sweden, thence to Gothenburg and Oslo, where they arrived on 30 September. Oslo was entered amid scenes of great enthusiasm and at this, the end of the line, the team had covered 4,958 miles, including 1,265 miles in the ISDT.

Perhaps of all the events of the 1950s this epic performance not only recalls all that was best about the ISDT in its original form as a test of strength, stamina and performance of basic production roadsters, but also puts paid to any ideas about the poor reliability record of British bikes of the era.

1921 BSA 3½hp, 557cc, side valve single with belt final drive, 3 speed hand gear change, acetylene lighting, Tan Sad pillion.
£3,200–3,500 *BKS*

1926 BSA B28, 249cc.
£2,000–2,500 *BLM*
This vintage lightweight BSA is often called the Wedge Tank.

1929 BSA 3½hp, 557cc, overhead valve, hub-braked model, 3-speed hand change gearbox, good condition.
£2,900–3,200 *BKS*

Originally a munitions manufacturer, BSA moved into bicycle making in the late 1880s and built its first own-design motorcycle in 1910. The first model to feature the marque's distinctive green and cream tank colours was a 499cc sidevalve single. This was soon complemented by a 557cc version, built initially with single speed belt drive transmission, and later on with a 3 speed gearbox and chain drive. The company's first overhead valve machine, a racer intended to bring TT honours to Small Heath, proved a dismal failure, but the acquisition of Daimler designer Harold Briggs resulted in a neat 350 overhead valve single capable of 70mph. Larger versions followed.

1929 BSA Sloper, 499cc, concours condition.
£2,500–3,500 *PC*

First sold in 1927, the Sloper became one of BSA's more popular models, gaining an excellent reputation for reliability and high mileage.

1933 BSA Blue Star, 349cc, sporty overhead valve twin port engine, hi-level exhaust, girder forks and rigid frame.
£2,500–3,000 *BLM*

1930 BSA Sloper, 493cc, forged steel spine frame, chromium-plated brightwork, twin port cylinder heads, 3-speed hand change gearbox, pillion seat, restored, good condition.
£4,500–5,000 *BKS*

1934 BSA Model B2, 249cc long stroke engine, green and chrome petrol tank, black paintwork and electric headlamp, good condition.
£850–1,000 *BKS*

1934 BSA B34-2, 249cc overhead valve engine, rigid frame, girder front forks, 3-speed hand change gearbox, full electrical system.
£1,200–1,400 *BKS*

l. **1934 BSA BI,** 249cc side valve single, hand gear change, older restoration, good condition.
£1,600–1,900 *AT*

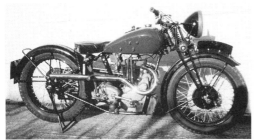

1936 BSA Blue Star, 499cc, overhead valve single cylinder, 4-stroke, bore and stroke 85 x 88mm, 23bhp.
£3,000–3,500 *AT*

This model was the largest version of the long running Blue Star range and continued the BSA tradition of building motorcycles of simple and inexpensive design.

1936 BSA Model G14, 1000cc side valve V-twin engine, hand gear change, footboards, Siamesed exhaust.
£5,000–6,000 *BLM*

This powerful V-twin made an ideal sidecar lugger.

r. **1937 BSA Empire Star B24,** 349cc, good condition.
£2,000–2,250 *PM*

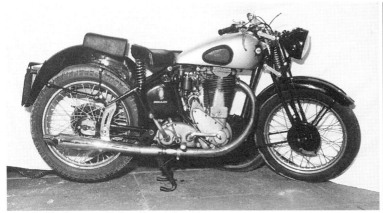

1949 BSA Gruppo Velox Special, 499cc.
£2,500–3,000 *NLM*

This motorcyle is the only known example of some 5 complete machines built by the Italian Parena concern, the engineering arm of Gruppo Velox. This BSA M20 based engine was made mainly for Motocross and general competition work. The manufacturers were highly regarded for their overhead valve systems for BSA and several other manufacturers of side valve engines in the 1940s. About 75 motors each individually numbered were based on BSA. A sort of pre-date Saturno/Gold Star. Tested in the 1940s at over 110mph and with superbly crafted Guzzi-style rear suspension.

1946 BSA C10, 249cc side valve single, iron head and barrel.
£800–1,400 *BLM*

In April 1946 the C-range received hydraulically damped, telescopic front forks. At the same time, the speedometer was transferred into the tank top – copied from the larger B-range in both aspects.

1945 BSA C10, 249cc side valve single, rigid frame and girder forks, speedo mounted next to headlamp.
£800–1,400 *VIN*

1946 BSA C10, 249cc, restored to high standard.
£1,500–2,000 *BKS*

BSA's C-range of lightweight machines was introduced in 1938. Similar in many ways to those of the larger B-range, whose wheels and brakes were employed, the cycle parts consisted of a simple diamond frame and girder front fork. The first model was the C10 side valve single with coil ignition and 3-speed hand change gearbox. A de luxe C10 with foot change gearbox joined the range in 1939, as did the overhead valve C11. When the C10 re-appeared after the war, its oil was no longer contained in a fuel tank compartment, but in a separate tank bolted to the saddle tube. The girder fork was replaced by a telescopic unit in mid-1946, and part way through 1949 an alloy cylinder head was adopted. The model ran on as the updated C10L, with alternator electrics, plunger rear suspension, and 4-speed gearbox until 1957.

1947 BSA B32, 348cc, overhead valve single cylinder engine, iron head and barrel, 4-speed, telescopic forks and rigid frame.
£2,000–2,250 *AT*

1947 BSA B31, 348cc, overhead single cylinder.
£1,800–2,000 *PM*

1948 BSA A7, 495cc, overhead valve twin, 62 x 82mm, 26bhp at 6000rpm, recently restored.
£2,000–3,000 *PC*

The first A7 appeared in 1946, and this 1948 model is virtually identical. Features include rigid frame, handlebar mounted speedo (tank mounted on earlier model) and telescopic forks.

Don't Forget!
If in doubt please refer to the 'How to Use' section at the beginning of this book.

l. **1947 BSA M20,** 496cc.
£1,450–1,650 *PM*

The BSA model range in the first austere months after the end of WWII saw the company offer not only the C10/C11 250s, but the overhead valve B31 and the side valve M20.

1949 BSA D1 Bantam, 123cc.
£750–1,000 *PM*

In June 1948 one of the best known of all BSA models made its debut as the Bantam. This single piston port 2-stroke became their best ever selling model, and sold in vast numbers all around the world. Interestingly, the engine was very much a copy of the pre-war DKW RT125.

1949 BSA B33, 499cc.
£2,000–2,200 *AT*

The year of 1949 brought more new models from the BSA empire and improved features for existing ones. Foremost among the latter was the option of plunger rear suspension for the twin and the B-range singles.

1951 BSA M20 Civilian Model, 496cc side valve single cylinder, bore and stroke 82 x 94mm, original condition.
£1,200–1,800 *CROW*

1950 BSA C10, 249cc side valve single cylinder, plunger rear suspension and pillion pad.
£800–1,000 *PS*

1951 BSA B34 Gold Star, 499cc.
£4,000–4,500 *BLM*

The first post-war Gold Star was the B32 GS in 1949 and by 1951 had been joined by the larger engined version.

1951 BSA B32 Gold Star, 348cc, superbly restored plunger frame Gold Star.
£3,500–4,000 *BLM*

l. **1952 BSA A10 Golden Flash,** 646cc.
£2,000–2,500 *BLM*

BSA's first post-war twin, the 495cc A7, arrived in 1949, followed a year later by the A10 Golden Flash. On the surface this was an enlarged A7, but in fact the engines were heavily revised, using the A7 only as a starting point. Few parts remained common, the most obvious concerned the cylinder head where the rocker box became a one-piece affair and the inlet manifold was cast as part of the head.

1952 BSA D1 Bantam, 123cc.
£800–1,000 *BLM*

This is a popular learner bike.

1952 BSA ZB32 Gold Star, 348cc.
£3,450–3,850 *BKS*

The fame of the BSA Gold Star lies with its dominance of the Isle of Man Clubman's races during the 1950s. In 1952 the Gold Star was still designated as being in the ZB range and this was the last year it was fitted with a plunger frame. There was for this year a new Bert Hopwood engine design involving a separate rocker box and modified cylinder head and barrel which at the time made the machine very competitive. That year 100 machines were prepared for entry into the Clubman's race on the island and this is almost certainly one of those machines.

l. **1953 BSA B31,** 348cc.
£1,500–1,750 *PM*

The B31/B33 gained the option of a dual seat for 1952 and the following year saw a headlamp cowl plus, only for the B33, an 8in front brake.

1953 BSA M21, 596cc.
£1,500–1,700 *BLM*

This big version of the BSA side valve single was ideal for sidecar use.

1953 BSA B31, 348cc, overhead valve single cylinder, plunger frame, 4-speed foot change.
£1,500–1,800 *MAY*

1954 BSA M33, 499cc, fully restored, concours condition.
£2,400–2,800 *BOC*

The M33 model was produced by fitting the overhead valve B33 engine into the heavy duty cycle parts shared by the M20/21 side valve machines.

1954 BSA C10L, 249cc, tidy restoration, 63 x 80mm bore and stroke.
£900–950 *AT*

1954 BSA A10, 646cc, Siamesed exhaust with Gold Star silencer, period rear carrier, otherwise standard model.
£1,700–1,900 *AT*

c1955 BSA B31, 348cc, café racer conversion with clip-ons, rear sets footrests, swept back pipe, Goldie silencer, alloy guards.
£1,700–2,000 *BLM*

1955 BSA Bantam Major, 148cc.
£300–375 *AT*

This is a larger bore version of original D1 (57 instead of 52), stroke unchanged at 58mm.

1955 BSA C12, 249cc, overhead valve, 4-speed, swinging arm frame, concours condition, fully restored.
£1,200–1,400 *AT*

For 1955 the C range changed to alternator electrics.

1956 BSA DB34, 499cc, Gold Star in Clubman's trim, alloy wheel rims, Amal concentric carburettors and V-shape headlamp brackets.
£6,000–6,250 *AT*

1956 BSA B31, 348cc.
£1,600–1,700 *BLM*

The 1956 B31 retained its 1945-type engine with little change, but now had a new frame, tank, seat and Ariel wheels.

l. **1956 BSA DB34 Gold Star,** 499cc, overhead valve, single cylinder, close ratio RRT2 gearbox.
£5,000–6,000 *CROW*

Ex-racer fitted with many Eddie Dow accessories.

1956 BSA M21, 596cc, side valve, single
bore, 4-stroke, 82 x 112mm bore and stroke,
plunger frame.
£1,250–1,650 *AT*

1957 BSA A10 Golden Flash, 646cc, overhead
valve twin.
£2,800–3,000 *BLM*

*This machine in an ideal all-round period big twin
with correct Ariel type full width hubs and brakes.*

1957 BSA A10 Golden Flash, 646cc,
largely standard except Gold Star silencers,
headlamp and instrument layout.
£2,000–2,500 *PS*

1957 BSA Bantam Major, 148cc, swinging arm frame.
£700–800 *PS*

1957 BSA A10 Road Rocket, 646cc, sports twin
with alloy big valve head, rev counter and Ariel
type hubs.
£2,900–3,300 *BLM*

1958 BSA A7 Special, 497cc.
£1,750–2,000 *PS*

*Although the original A7 twin was designed by
Herbert Perkins, the later models were improved
by Bert Hopwood at the time when his Golden
Flash was introduced. This machine is fitted with
stainless steel mudguards, otherwise largely to the
maker's original specification.*

1958 BSA A10 Special, 646cc.
£1,650–2,000 *PS*

This machine is a mixture of several models.

1959 BSA DB32 Gold Star Clubman, 348cc.
£6,500–7,000 *BLM*

It was the 350, rather than the 500 Gold Star which had the most success in the Clubman TT on the Isle of Man. It is also a much smoother bike to ride.

1959 BSA D7 Bantam Super, 172cc,
piston port 2 stroke.
£290–320 *BKS*

The first of the 175 Bantam was the D5, followed 2 years later by the D7.

1960 BSA DBD34 Gold Star Clubman, 499cc,
modifications include modern tyres on alloy rims,
twin leading shoe conversion for 190mm front
brake, Amal concentric carburettor, fly screen and
belt primary drive on a Norton Commando clutch,
standard BSA gearbox.
£6,000–7,000 *BLM*

1961 BSA A10 Super Rocket, 647cc,
overhead valve twin, converted to
12 volt electrics and electronic ignition.
£4,000–4,250 *BLM*

> **Miller's is a price GUIDE
> not a price LIST**

r. **1961 BSA Super Rocket,**
646cc, concours condition, fully
restored to original specification.
£3,000–3,300 *AT*

1962 BSA C15 Star, 247cc, overhead valve unit single cylinder.
£850–1,000 *MAY*

The C15 was launched in September 1958 and was to become the basis for an entire unit construction range. Ignition points in housing behind the cylinder distinguish the early models which remained unchanged in touring guise for several years.

1962 BSA A50, 499cc, overhead valve, 4-speed, 28.5bhp at 6000rpm.
£1,200–1,400 *BKS*

Introduced in January 1962, the A50 and larger A65 were BSA's replacements for the well respected A7 and A10 models. The newcomers featured unit construction engines and gearboxes. Despite the modern appearance and fine handling, they never gained the popularity that their predecessors or competitors enjoyed.

1963 BSA D7 Bantam, 175cc.
£400–500 *S*

The ubiquitous Bantam needs little introduction other than to confirm that with over 400,000 produced it was, by far, the largest selling machine from any British manufacturer during its 15 year lifespan.

Locate the Source

The source of each illustration in Miller's can be found by checking the code letters below each caption with the Key to Illustrations.

l. **1964 BSA D1 Bantam GPO Model,** 123cc.
£1,000–1,200 *PC*

For many years the GPO used the D1 Bantam for telegram and other vital deliveries.

l. **1964 BSA A65 Star,** 654cc.
£2,800–3,200 *BLM*
New for 1962, the A65 Star twin had a unit construction engine, 75 x 74mm bore and stroke dimensions, a compression ratio of 7.5:1 and a power output of 38bhp at 5800rpm. Maximum speed was just over 100mph.

1963 BSA B40, 343cc.
£850–1,000 *MAY*
The B40 was introduced for 1961. It was very similar to the C15, but there was no separate pushrod tube, 18in wheels and 7in front brake.

1964 BSA Beagle, 74.7cc.
£115–125 *BKS*
Announced in the autumn of 1962 and intended as a replacement for the D1 Bantam, the flyweight Beagle commenced production the following year. Powered by a single cylinder 4 stroke engine (as used in the Ariel Pixie scooter in 49cc form), the Beagle could cruise at 40mph and achieve 150mpg. Unfortunately for BSA, competition from Honda's faster and better equipped step-thru models meant that sales were disappointing, and the Beagle was withdrawn in 1965. This example is substantially original and complete, and is equipped with optional legshields and carrier.

1964 BSA SS80, 247cc.
£1,000–1,500 *BKS*
This was the final year of distributor ignition before the points were moved to a new location in the timing chest. By 1964 there were various forms of the C15, including the SS80 sports model. The 1964 SS80 had an 8:1 compression ratio, blade mudguards, light alloy fork shrouds and a 16 tooth gearbox sprocket to liven up performance. This particular machine has been fitted with mirrors, indicators and a top box for every day riding.

1967 BSA A50 Royal Star, 499cc, overhead valve unit twin, single carburettor, with export tank and bars.
£2,000–2,300 *BLM*

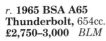

r. **1965 BSA A65 Thunderbolt,** 654cc.
£2,750–3,000 *BLM*
The single carburettor Thunderbolt, one of the best of BSA's unit twins as it remained in tune much longer than twin carb variants.

1967 BSA A65L Lightning, 654cc, overhead valve
twin, dual carburettors.
£2,000–2,700 *CONQ*

*This example has the smaller export fuel tank from
an earlier model and non-standard silencers.*

1967 BSA B25 Starfire, 247cc.
£1,250–1,450 *BLM*

*The B25 Starfire and C25 Barracuda were both
new for 1967. The engine benefited from experience
gained with the Victor motocrosser.*

1967 BSA D10 Bantam, 172cc.
£525–625 *PS*

*Introduced in 1966 with points on right, alternator
with improved output, more power and 4 plate clutch.*

1968 BSA Spitfire MkIV, 654cc.
£2,300–2,500 *BKS*

1968 BSA D14 Bantam, 172cc, fully restored,
concours condition.
£1,200–1,300 *BRIT*

1968 BSA Bantam D14/4, 172cc.
£670–720 *BKS*

Introduced in 1968, the 3 new D14/4 models all featured 4-speed gearboxes, whilst minor tuning tweaks, notably an increase in compression, resulted in a power output approaching 14bhp.

1969 BSA A65 Thunderbolt, 654cc, single carburettor, concours condition.
£3,400–3,700 *BRIT*

1969 BSA D175 Bantam, 172cc, standard except Motoplas screen, top box and carrier.
£480–520 *HOLL*

r. **1972 BSA B50 GP Replica,** 499cc, overhead valve single cylinder, 4-speed, street legal, new components, nearly new engine.
£3,500–4,000 *CROW*

1968 BSA Starfire, 247cc, single cylinder, air-cooled, overhead valve 4-stroke.
£680–740 *BKS*

BSA eventually phased out their 250cc C15 range in favour of a 250cc hot single specifically designed for the American market and called the Starfire. Edward Turner had been in the States and upon his return he decided that the development of the C25 Starfire would reach a potentially strong American market and he even rejected further progress on a Hopwood design triple 250cc in favour of the new generation of 250s.

This machine is a single cylinder, air-cooled, 250cc overhead valve 4 stroke with a higher compression and hotter cams than previous models. It has a sculptured tank and side panels.

1970 BSA B25 Starfire, 247cc.
£1,200–1,300 *MAY*

r. **1971 BSA A65 Firebird Scrambler,** 654cc, overhead valve twin cylinder, dual Amal concentric carburettors.
£2,500–3,500 *CONQ*

For 1971 the Firebird Scrambler received new frame, forks and wheels. Built for export only, it was essentially a Lightning with scrambles modifications for the North American market.

CALTHORPE *(British 1911–39)*

1936 Calthorpe Ivory, 348cc, overhead valve, twin port single cylinder, 3-speed footchange gearbox.
£2,500–2,700 *BKS*

The Calthorpe factory restyled their machines in 1928 adopting an ivory coloured paint scheme for their tank and mudguards, hence the ivory prefix to their product name. The factory was never a strong contender on the racing scene but nevertheless they made a range of solid well-engineered products during the first half of the 1930s. Their last appearance at the Earl's Court Show was in 1934 where they displayed models in 250, 350 and 500cc capacities. Thereafter their fortunes diminished and in 1938 they went into liquidation and the company was purchased by Bruce Douglas a member of the Bristol Douglas family. Unfortunately, before the name could be revived the commencement of WWII stopped production and thereafter the name disappeared.

CLYNO *(British 1911–24)*

1919 Clyno Single, 249cc, single cylinder, piston port 2-stroke, hand gearchange.
£1,900–2,000 *PS*

COTTON *(British 1919–80)*

1926 Cotton TT Model 29, 349cc, Blackburne overhead valve engine.
£4,500–5,000 *COEC*

COVENTRY EAGLE *(British 1901–39)*

1926 Coventry Eagle Flying Eight, 986cc, overhead valve, narrow angle V-twin engine.
£6,000–7,000 *BKS*

Originally a bicycle manufacturer, Coventry Eagle built a diverse range of machines using proprietary engines from 1901–39. Most famous of all was the Flying Eight, with its 1 litre overhead valve JAP V-twin engine and muscular good looks. It was a worthy rival for the Brough-Superior, and a formidable Brooklands racing machine.

CZ *(Czechoslovakian 1932–)*

Originally an armaments manufacturer, the Czech firm of CZ diversified into motorcycle production in the early 1930s. CZ's operations were combined with those of erstwhile rival Jawa in 1949, and throughout the 1950s and '60s the marque's main claim to fame was an outstanding run of success in the ISDT and in international motocross. It was commuter machines, though, which formed the mainstay of CZ production. Launched in 1968, the type 477, 172cc 2-stroke proved very popular in the UK. Equipped with Posilube pumped lubrication and driving through a 4 speed gearbox, the ruggedly built single produced a claimed 15bhp at 5600rpm, an output good enough for a top speed of 75mph. More important to the prospective CZ customer though, was the 80+ miles per gallon fuel consumption.

1973 CZ 175 Roadster, 172cc.
£350–450 *BKS*

DOUGLAS *(British 1906–57)*

The Bristol-based Douglas Foundry took up motorcycle production in 1907 with a machine powered by a horizontally-opposed twin, and the company would kept faith with this engine layout until it ceased motorcycle production in 1957. Fore-and-aft installation made for a slim machine with a low centre of gravity, and the design's virtues were soon demonstrated in competition, Douglas machines taking first, second and fourth places in the 1912 Junior TT in the Isle of Man. Douglas were quick to realise the advantages of the countershaft gearbox, its 3-speed entries gaining the Team Prize in the 1914 Six Days Trial, a conspicuous success which resulted in the firm obtaining a wartime contract for the supply of military machines.

1912 Douglas Flat Twin 2¾hp, 348cc.
£6,500–7,000 *BKS*

During the early part of 1912 the Bristol Douglas factory became associated with the Williamson marque. It was also in 1912 that the factory achieved its first success by winning the TT race in the Isle of Man and another of their machines, in the same race was also accredited with the fastest lap.

r. **1919 Douglas 2¾hp Model V,** 348cc.
£4,600–5,000 *BKS*

Described in contemporary advertising as 'the business man's ideal mount possessed of that ease of control and turn of speed which is the making of a perfect touring machine'. The Douglas 2¾hp had, of course, been well proven in military service in WWI, its 348cc engine proving durable in adverse conditions and in the hands of novice riders.

1914 Douglas 2¾hp, 348cc, fore-and-aft horizontally opposed twin cylinder engine, belt final drive.
£5,500–6,000 *BLM*

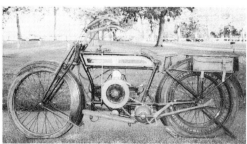

1920 Douglas 2¾hp W20, 348cc.
£3,700–4,000 *BKS*

1920 Douglas W20, 348cc.
£4,600–4,800 *VER*

Did you know?

Miller's Collectors Classic Motorcycles
Price Guide *builds up year-by-year to
form the most comprehensive photo
library system available.*

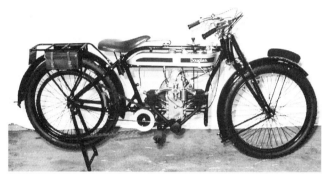

1924 Douglas T5, 348cc.
£3,500–4,000 *BKS*

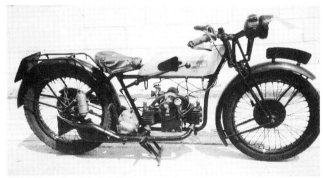

1929 Douglas Model EW, 348cc, flat twin, needing restoration.
£1,200–1,400 *AT*

1957 Douglas Dragonfly, 348cc.
£2,600–3,000 *BKS*

The Dragonfly arrived in 1955 and featured a revised engine
with stronger crank case, single carburettor, and updated
electrics and ignition. The duplex frame employed a
conventional swinging arm with Girling dampers in place of the
preceding torsion bar arrangement, while the Radiadraulic front
fork gave way to an Earles-type leading link set-up.

1926 Douglas Model EW, 348cc.
£2,700–3,000 *BKS*

*Designed by Cyril Pullin and launched
at the Olympia Show in 1925, the EW
model was intended to benefit from the
road tax concessions available to
lightweights, and so weighed in at less
than 200lbs. In typical Douglas fashion
the newcomer's power unit was a fore-
and-aft flat twin; in EW form a fixed-
head side valve with outside flywheel,
hand and mechanical oil pumps, and
BTH magneto ignition. A gearbox
mounted behind rather than above the
rear cylinder, all-chain drive, and
decent sized drum brakes differentiated
the EW from its predecessors. An
unusual feature was the gearchange
gate in the centre of the petrol tank.
Early examples gained a reputation for
unreliability, but the works made
numerous improvements and the model
went on to achieve some notable
successes in the popular reliability
trials of the period.*

1948 Douglas MkIV, 348cc.
£3,450–3,850 *BKS*

*Douglas commenced post-war
production in 1947 with, naturally
enough, a flat twin, though unlike the
vast majority of previous models the
T35 mounted its engine across the
frame. The former was of unit
construction, while the latter displayed
even greater innovation with its
swinging arm rear suspension
controlled by torsion bars, and leading
link Radiadraulic front fork. After
development work had cured frame
breakages and improved engine power,
the revised version was dubbed the
MkIII. The latter lasted until the
advent of the new for 1949 MkIV
version, which featured an unsprung
front mudguard and altered rear
subframe with distinctive teardrop-
shaped toolboxes.*

DUCATI *(Italian 1946–)*

1961 Ducati 200 Elite, 204cc, overhead camshaft
single cylinder, 4-speed, wet sump lubrication.
£2,000–2,500 *PC*

1964 Ducati 250 Mach 1, 248cc, overhead
camshaft single cylinder, 29mm Dell'Orto SS ID
carburettor, 5-speed, concours condition.
£3,000–3,500 *PC*

*Standard except optional alloy rims, also straight
instead of curved kickstart lever. Together with
Suzuki T20 Super Six, the Mach 1 was the worlds
first production 250 to top 100mph in road trim.*

1962 Ducati USA Spec 250 Diana.
£3,400–3,500 *PC*

*This motorcycle is a very rare original Diana
MkIII, in absolutely pristine condition. The
majority of these models ended their days as
racing machines.*

1966 Ducati USA MkIII, 248cc,
excellent condition.
£2,000–2,200 *DUC*

1966 Ducati Monza Junior, 156cc.
£800–1,000 *IMO*

*Square styling did not suit everyone's taste, but it
still had an excellent overhead camshaft bevel
single cylinder motor and good handling.*

r. **1967 Ducati Sebring,** 340cc, finished in silver
with black frame, one owner, 658 miles from new,
upswept handlebars, period accessory mirror, and
tower luggage rack.
£1,100–1,250 *BKS*

1971 Ducati 450 MkIII, 436cc, overhead camshaft bevel single cylinder, 5-speed, wet-sump lubrication, matching speedo and tacho, full width alloy hubs, valve lifter, Silentium silencer and touring bars.
£2,000–2,200 *DUC*

1972 Ducati 23 Horas, 246cc, built in Barcelona, Spain at the Mototrans factory, 5-speed, narrowcase engine, different bore and stroke to Italian models.
£1,800–2,000 *PC*

1973 Ducati 450 SCR Desmo, 436cc, rare model with Desmo cylinder head and Borrani alloy rims, Italian import, non-standard headlamp, 18in front wheel rim and tyre.
£1,800–2,000 *DUC*

l. **1972 Ducati Scrambler 450,** 436cc, original condition, specification includes valve lifter, heavyweight 35mm Marzocchi front forks and rear shock rubber gaiters.
£2,000–2,300 *PC*

1974 Ducati Desmo Drum 450, 436cc.
£3,200–3,400 *IMO*

Ducati offered buyers the choice of either Marzocchi forks/Grimeca double-sided drum or Ceriani forks/Brembo single disc.

1974 Ducati 450 MkIII, 436cc, overhead camshaft bevel single cylinder, 5-speed, electronic ignition, concours condition.
£2,500–3,000 *PC*

This particular MkIII has been customised with fairing, Cernan & McKay cast alloy wheel conversion, rear sets, plus Desmo model parts, including seat.

1974 Ducati 250 Desmo Drum, 248cc.
£2,700–2,900 *IMO*

1974 Ducati 250 MkIII, 248cc, non-standard
yellow/black paintwork, earlier model headlamp
and tail lamp.
£1,600–1,800 *DUC*

1974 Ducati 750SS, 748cc.
£7,000–8,000 *PC*

*One of the very rare, round case 750SS Imola
replica Desmo V-twins. This one has optional
hi-level exhaust, but is lacking original side panels
and rear mudguard. Non-standard paintwork with
silver bodywork and red frame.*

> **Miller's is a price GUIDE
> not a price LIST**

l. **1974 Ducati 750 Sport,** 748cc, late model with
central axle forks, dual seat and polished outer
engine covers.
£4,500–5,000 *PC*

r. **1975 Ducati
900SS,** 864cc,
concours condition.
£5,000–5,500 *CARS*

*This is one of the first
batch of the famous 900
Super Sport models
which were hand-built
for the initial batch in
1975. Special features
of these early machines
included fibreglass
Imola fuel tank and
right-hand gearchange.
This example is pristine
but missing side panels.*

1977 Ducati 500 Sport Desmo, 498cc, Desmo parallel twin, totally original, low mileage.
£2,000–2,200 *PC*

1978 Ducati Darmah SD900, 864cc, overhead camshaft V-twin with Desmodromic valve operation.
£2,200–2,600 *IMO*

The Darmah was Ducati's first attempt to internationalise their machines and featured Bosch headlamp and part electrical system, the remainder of the electrical equipment being provided by Nippon Denso, including the switchgear. Other features included cast alloy wheels, Brembo brakes and stainless steel mudguards. Maximum speed 122mph.

l. **1979 Ducati 350 GTV,** 349cc, overhead camshaft with chain drive, 5-speed gearbox, cast alloy wheels, triple disc brakes, finished in black and gold, concours condition.
£1,600–1,800 *DUC*

1979 Ducati 350 GTV, 349cc, chain driven overhead camshaft parellel twin, standard machine except for silencers.
£1,500–1,600 *PC*

1979 Ducati 900SS, 864cc, good condition.
£4,500–5,000 *IMO*

1979 Ducati 900SS, 864cc, standard except pillion grabrail and rider's mirror.
£4,500–4,800 *PC*

1980 Ducati SD Sport Darmah MkII, 864cc,
40mm carburettors and Silentium silencers,
completely original.
£2,400–2,600 *PC*

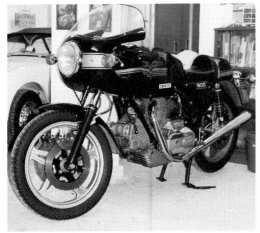

1982 Ducati 900SS, 864cc.
£4,000–4,500 *DUC*

*Last of the 900SS bevel V-twins before the launch
of the 900S2 in 1983.*

1980 Ducati 900SS, 864cc,
original, very low mileage.
£4,700–5,000 *PC*

r. **1982 Ducati 600SL Pantah,** 583cc.
£2,500–2,800 *PC*

*Finished in Italian home market colours of red,
white and green – as Mike Hailwood replica.
Export models were usually silver.*

r. **1984 Ducati Mike
Hailwood Replica,** 864cc.
£4,200–4,400 *IMO*

*Last of '900' 864cc MHR
models with square engine
covers and non-standard
2-into-1 exhaust system.*

EXCELSIOR *(British 1886–1964)*

1937 Excelsior Manxman, 349cc, overhead camshaft single cylinder engine.
£8,000–8,500 *BKS*

1917 Excelsior Blackburne, 325cc, 2-stroke single cylinder engine.
£1,600–1,900 *BKS*

The origins of Excelsior lay with the Bayliss Thomas partnership who originally made bicycles and then fitted Minerva engines to them at the very dawn of the motorcycle industry in this country in about 1896. By WWI, although showing interest in sporting events, they proceeded to manufacture ever larger single cylinder machines, one model being of an incredible 5.6hp.

Produced in 250, 350 and 500cc capacities this overhead camshaft single cylinder sports machine is always a reminder of the factory's success in racing both at home at the Manx Grand Prix and on the Continent during the latter half of the 1930s. The 350 was especially reliable with an engine design incorporating 2 valves operated from the overhead camshaft with an extra large crankshaft assembly which provided renowned reliability for many sporting riders up to the end of the 1930s.

FB MONDIAL *(Italian 1948–79)*

FN *(Belgium 1901–57)*

1948 FN Model XIII, 450cc, side valve single cylinder, foot change gearbox.
£1,600–2,000 *BLM*

1955 FB Mondial Constellation 200, 198cc.
£1,500–1,700 *PC*

The overhead valve Constellation featured a 4-speed gearbox and was intended as a touring, rather than sports machine. The machine's most unusual feature was its forward operating kickstart, located on the offside of the machine.

FRANCIS-BARNETT
(British 1919–64)

1962 Francis-Barnett Cruiser 89, 249cc, 2-stroke Villiers 2T twin cylinder engine.
£700–800 *PS*

1923 Francis-Barnett, 150cc, 2-stroke single cylinder.
£900–1,000 *PM*

r. **1963 Francis-Barnett Falcon 87,** 199cc, 2-stroke AMC single cylinder engine.
£450–550 *PS*

GILERA *(Italian 1909–)*
110 Years of Gilera

The famous Italian marque was founded by Giuseppe Gilera, who was born on 21 December 1887 at Zelobuonpersico, a small village to the south-east of Milan.

Gilera's fame came from its involvement with European racing in the early/mid-1950s, when every factory of any consequence ran an équipe of talented riders and tuning experts.

This period was marked by a battle for supremacy between the established 4-stroke single and the up-and-coming multi. And it was the Gilera four, ridden by stars such as Geoff Duke, Bob McIntyre and Libero Liberati, that won in the end.

The design, however, had its roots in the inter-war days and first appeared in the early 1930s as CNA's Rome-built Rondine four. A water-cooled, supercharged 500 producing 60bhp at 8500rpm, the design began in real style by winning its first ever race, the 1935 Tropoli Grand Prix, in the hands of the legendary Piero Taruffi.

At the end of that year Gilera purchased the blueprints, and the model was given an all-enveloping shell for record attempts, highlights being Taruffi's world 500cc effort of 170.37mph during 1937 and, two years later, his hour record of 127 miles, set on a 28-mile stretch of the Bergamo-Brescia autostrada.

Also in 1939, Dorini Serafini became European 500cc champion with a 97.85mph victory in the Ulster GP, then the world's fastest road race thanks to the eight-mile-long Clady straight.

After the hostilities, and to conform to the FIM's post-war ban on supercharging, Pietro Remor redesigned the Gilera into an air-cooled, 4-carb, 5-speed stallion which ultimately gave 70bhp at 10,500rpm.

The world championship series was inaugurated in 1949, with Umberto Massetti winning the blue riband 500cc class in 1950 and 1952 with Norton-mounted Geoff Duke taking the crown in 1951.

By the end of 1952 even Duke's supreme riding skills could not offset the Gilera speed advantage, and so the Englishman switched to the Italian squad. Working in tandem with Taruffi on development, he notched up a brilliant hat-trick of world titles and gave the Italian company its first Senior TT victory in 1955.

But it was that great Scot, Bob McIntyre, selected by Duke as a replacement when he himself was injured at Imola in 1956, who lifted Gilera to their greatest ever moment during the swansong year of racing, 1957. Commencing with a Junior TT victory, McIntyre then simply ran away with the eight-lap (307 mile) Golden Jubilee Senior TT, notching the first ever 100 mile an hour TT lap in the process.

A neck injury stopped McIntyre winning the championship but not from stretching the hour record to 141 miles on Monza's diabolically bumpy banked course – deliberately opting to ride the smaller 350 four so that he could keep the throttle pinned and thus concentrate his effort on his marathon wrestling match.

What a way for a factory to quit the speed scene!

1939 Gilera 500 Supercharged Racer, 499cc.
£250,000+ *PC*

This is one of a handful of pre-war Gilera 4 cylinder supercharged racers. Dorino Serafina was European Champion on just such a machine in 1939.

1949 Gilera Nettuno Sport, 247cc, overhead valve single cylinder, 4-speed foot-operated gearchange, concours condition.
£2,000–2,500 *PC*

1950 Gilera Saturno Sport, 499cc, overhead valve single cylinder, 4-speed.
£5,500–6,000 *VMC(P)*

An uprated version of the Saturno Sport with telescopic forks was first shown at the Milan Show in 1950, and was launched early the following year.

1946 Gilera Nettuno Turismo, 247cc.
£1,500–2,000 *BKS*

Gilera was quick to commence post-war production but due to war shortages production was limited adding to the rarity of the very early post-war products from this factory. This machine is 4-stroke air-cooled, fitted at present with a straight through exhaust system, flat handlebars but no lighting equipment. It has a sprung pan seat and is fitted with a 4-speed gearbox.

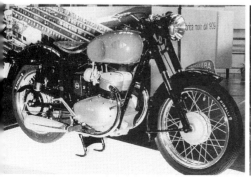

l. **1954 Gilera B300,** 304cc, overhead valve twin cylinders, parallel valves.
£1,500–1,650 *PC*

This is one of the first models with alloy silencers, single saddle and alloy wheel rims.

1956 Gilera 150 Sport, 149cc, overhead valve
single cylinder, 4-speed gearbox unit construction,
concours condition.
£1,100–1,200 *PC*

1956 Gilera 150 Sport, 149cc,
overhead valve single cylinder,
in need of restoration.
£400–500 *MAY*

Locate the Source
*The source of each
illustration in Miller's
can be found by checking
the code letters below
each caption with the
Key to Illustrations.*

r. **1961 Gilera 125 Six Days,** 124cc.
£800–1,000 *PC*

1959 Gilera 175 Rossa Extra,
174cc, overhead valve single cylinder.
£1,500–1,600 *PC*

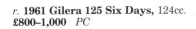

1977 Gilera Trial, 49cc, piston port 2-stroke
single cylinder, 4-speed sports
moped/lightweight motorcycle.
£300–400 *PC*

GREEVES *(British 1952–78)*

1968 Greeves 24 DF Police, 249cc, 2-stroke
Villiers 4T twin cylinder engine.
£900–1,000 *GRA*

1929 AJS Model 9, 498cc.
£2,750–3,000 *BLM*

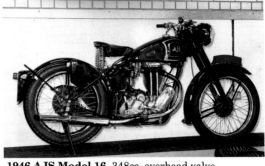

1946 AJS Model 16, 348cc, overhead valve, single saddle, AMC telescopic forks, black finish, with gold pinstriping.
£1,500–2,000 *CONQ*

1953 AJS Model 16MS, 349cc, overhead valve engine, 4-speed gearbox, chain primary drive, full width hubs, valenced mudguards.
£2,000–2,300 *BLM*

1955 AJS Model 18S, 497cc, overhead valve single, recent complete restoration, unused since.
£2,250–2,500 *PS*

1955 AJS Model 20, 498cc, overhead valve twin cylinder engine, 4-speed gearbox, 'jampot' rear suspension units, full width brake hubs.
£2,300–2,500 *BLM*

1960 AJS Model 14, 248cc, overhead valve single, unit construction engine, fully restored to original specification.
£1,300–1,500 *WEED*

1964 AJS Model 14 CSR, 248cc.
£1,200–1,500 *AMOC*

Chrome-plated mudguards and tank are visual differences to the standard Model 14, but engine also in higher state of tune. Ridden by Peter Williams and Tony Wood, a similar example won the 250cc class of the 1964 Thruxton 500 mile endurance race.

1961 AJS Model 31 CSR, 646cc.
£2,800–3,000 *BLM*

This is a sportier version of the standard Model 31, with alloy mudguards and 2-into-1 exhaust.

1929 Ariel Model A, 550cc, side valve single cylinder, with girder forks, luggage carrier, full period electric lighting set, 'Brooklands' type fishtail exhaust and hand gearchange.
£2,100–2,300 *BKS*

1946 Ariel NG Red Hunter, 346cc, overhead valve single cylinder, 4-speeds, rigid frame, telescopic front forks, twin exhaust ports, fully restored.
£1,300–1,500 *TDC*

1947 Ariel NH Red Hunter, 346cc, good condition.
£1,400–1,600 *VMC(P)*

1951 Ariel Red Hunter, 499cc, 63 x 80mm bore and stroke.
£1,250–1,450 *BLM*

1955 Ariel VH, 499cc, overhead valve single cylinder, 4-speed, 26bhp at 6000rpm, concours condition, fully restored.
£2,500–2,800 *ABT*

The VH with swinging arm rear suspension was built from 1954 until its demise in 1959.

1956 Ariel NH Red Hunter, 346cc.
£1,800–2,000 *BLM*

The NH Red Hunter was one of Ariel's best sellers in the immediate post-war period and was produced from 1945 through to the end of 1959. Swinging arm suspension arrived in 1954.

1958 Ariel FH Huntmaster, 647cc, twin cylinder, 35bhp at 5750rpm.
£1,950–2,150 *AT*

The Huntmaster twin was introduced in 1954 using a BSA derived engine (from the A10), but with certain Ariel features to give it a different appearance. The cycle parts were Ariel's own.

1959 Ariel LH Colt, 198cc, overhead valve single, plunger rear suspension, concours condition, full restoration.
£1,100–1,300 *PS*

The Colt engine with cross pushrods was based on that of the BSA C11G. This is one of the last Colts manufactured, as production ceased in 1959.

1960 Ariel Leader, 247cc, piston port, parallel twin cylinder, 2-stroke.
£1,300–1,500 *BLM*

1979 Benelli 125/2 Sport, 124cc.
£580–640 *NLM*

Probably the prettiest of all Benelli's 2-stroke roadsters. The model is easily identifiable by its upswept exhaust, bikini fairing, low handlebars, cast alloy wheels and oblong direction indicators.

1984 Bimota HB3, 1160cc.
£6,000–6,500 *IMO*

This HB3 has an oversize 1160cc Wisco race kit in place of the original 1100 engine size.

1960 BMW R50, 494cc.
£3,000–3,250 *BLM*

R50 was the touring model of the Earles forked BMW twin range. There was also a R50S 'sports' version with tuned engine, timed breather and hydraulic steering damper.

1972 Benelli Tornado, 642cc, overhead valve twin cylinder, 5-speed, unit construction, drum brakes.
£1,400–1,500 *PC*

1978 Bimota KB1, 1000cc.
£4,300–4,700 *PC*

The KB1 housed the 900 or 1000cc double overhead camshaft Kawasaki engines, and debuted at the Milan Show in November 1977. This model has non-standard green/yellow livery.

1985 Bimota DB1, 749cc.
£6,200–6,800 *PC*

First of the Ducati powered Bimotas, the DB1 saved the company from financial ruin. It was also built as a racer for twins events. It used a big bore version of the Pantah engine.

1976 BMW R60/6, 599cc, overhead valve twin cylinder, 73.5 x 70.6mm bore and stroke, 40bhp, 5-speeds, telescopic forks, 11,000 miles recorded, totally original condition.
£2,000–2,500 *CROW*

1925 Brough Superior SS80, 986cc, specially tuned JAP V-twin engine, Sturmey Archer 3-speed gearbox and Brampton Biflex forks.
£15,000–17,000 *VER*

This an early example from George Brough's Nottingham-based company.

1936 Brough Superior SS80, 986cc.
£11,000–13,000 *VER*

1950 BSA Bantam D1, 123cc, piston port 2-stroke, 3-speed gearbox.
£500–600 *BKS*

BSA's humble little Bantam was popular with a number of organisations, most notably the Post Office, and the AA, who recognised that lightweight machines in urban environments were more mobile and economical.

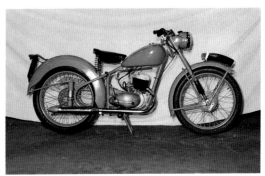

1953 BSA Bantam D3, 123cc, 2-stroke single cylinder, restored, good condition.
£325–425 *PS*

1948 BSA B31, 348cc, good condition.
£1,600–1,800 *BLM*

c1954 BSA B31, 348cc, overhead valve engine.
£1,150–1,250 *BKS*

BSA's rugged workaday B31 was manufactured from 1945 to 1959, its overhead valve engine providing the basis for the renowned Gold Star. Produced initially with a rigid frame, it was available from 1949 with optional plunger rear suspension, and switched to a swinging arm frame in 1954. Top speed was around 75mph, but the model's main attraction was its fuel economy, 100mpg being within reach of the careful rider.

1954 BSA A7 Shooting Star, 497cc, overhead valve twin, alloy cylinder head, concours condition, fully restored.
£2,700–3,000 *BOC*

This was the first year for this sporting version of A7 tourer.

1957 BSA A7, 497cc, correct Ariel brakes.
£2,300–2,600 *BLM*

1959 BSA A10, 646cc.
£2,700–2,900 *BLM*

The A10 carved an excellent reputation for reliability and was widely used for both solo and sidecar work.

1959 BSA D7, 172cc.
£500–600 *PS*

All 175 Bantams sported the swinging arm frame – unlike the smaller D1 (125) and D3 (150) models.

1961 BSA A7 Shooting Star, 497cc, overhead valve twin, alloy cylinder head, full width brakes, concours condition.
£2,800–3,200 *BLM*

1965 BSA C15, 247cc.
£800–1,200 *MAY*

In 1966 the SS80 became the C15 Sportsman. features included flat dual seat for one with a small hump at the rear, more swept-back handlebars, separate chrome-plated headlamp and standard ratios gears.

1966 BSA Spitfire Mark II, 654cc, finished in red, Amal GP carburettors.
£2,800–3,100 *BOC*

1968 BSA Spitfire MkIV, 654cc, export model with small tank.
£3,500–4,000 *BLM*

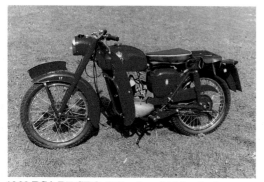

1968 BSA D7 GPO, 172cc, leg shields, single seat, carrier.
£1,000–1,200 *PC*

By 1968 the GPO were using the D7 175 Bantam, thus providing improved performance over the service's early D1 models.

1968 BSA Spitfire MkIV, 654cc, twin carburettors, twin leading shoe front brake.
£2,500–3,500 *CROW*

1935 Cotton 29/J, 349cc, JAP overhead valve engine, footchange, hi-level exhaust.
£3,500–4,000 *COEC*

1971 CZ 175S Model 477, 123cc, restored.
£250–350 *JCZ*

1980 CZ Monoshock Special, 124cc.
£400–500 *JCZ*

Special based on CZ commuter bike, but with monoshock rear suspension, Micron exhaust, hydraulic steering damper and clip-ons.

1926 Douglas Model EW, 348cc.
£1,150–1,350 *BKS*

Introduced in 1925 the new model EW from the Bristol factory incorporated many design changes including more efficient cooling fins on the cylinder casting, a new lubrication system and a general weight reduction to comply with the road tax arrangements of the day.

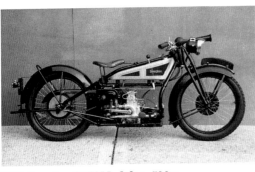

1926 Douglas OHV Modeloc, 596cc.
£7,000–8,000 *VER*

Larger version of Douglas's early twin with chain final drive.

1948 Douglas T35, 348cc, overhead valve horizontally opposed twin cylinder engine, shaft final drive.
£1,800–2,000 *BLM*

1950 Douglas 90 Plus, 348cc, overhead valve horizontal twin, shaft drive.
£3,400–3,700 *VER*

1951 Douglas MkV, 348cc, partly restored.
£1,650–1,850 *BLM*

1962 Ducati Daytona, 248cc.
£2,400–2,600 *IMO*

*Only known as the Daytona in the UK, elsewhere called
the Diana and in North America as the Diana MkIII.*

1964 Ducati Elite, 204cc.
£2,000–2,500 *IMO*

*The final Elites were constructed in 1963. However,
in several countries these remained available until
as late as 1965, due to existing stocks.*

1966 Ducati USA Spec MkIII, 248cc, Scrambler
front mudguard, alloy wheel rims.
£1,700–1,900 *PC*

One of a batch imported by Bill Hannah of Liverpool.

1971 Ducati 450 MkIII, 436cc.
£2,200–2,400 *PC*

*Later double-sided Grimeca drum brake, 900SS
(bevel) single seat, 1973/74 Aprilia headlamp,
alloy wheel rims, Hagon rear shocks, rear sets,
and several other non-standard features.*

1972 Ducati 450 SCR, 436cc, good condition.
£2,000–2,300 *PC*

1976 Ducati 860GTS, 864cc, overhead
camshaft, 90° V-twin.
£1,250–1,350 *BKS*

*This machine has Conti silencers (normally found
on the more sporting models), painted mudguards,
and cast alloy wheels from a post-1977 model.
However, the rear drum brake has been retained.*

1979 Ducati 900SS, 864cc, Desmodromic valve operation,
concours condition.
£4,000–4,400 *PC*

*Specially modified, nickel-plated frame, Lucas Rita
ignition, Brembo Gold Line calipers.*

1982 Ducati 500SL, 498cc, low mileage, pristine
condition, Conti-made 2-into-1 chrome exhaust.
£2,800–2,900 *PC*

The MkII version of 500SL with 600-type fairing.

1956 Francis-Barnett Plover, 149cc, 2-stroke, single cylinder Villiers engine, 3-speed gearbox.
£200–250 *PS*

1948 Gilera Saturno Sport, 499cc.
£5,500–6,000 *BLM*

First developed immediately prior to the outbreak of WWII, the Saturno became one of Gilera's best-loved models. It is often referred to as the 'Italian Gold Star'. Original model with girder forks.

1956 Gilera Sport, 172cc, overhead valve single, unit construction engine, alloy wheel rims, 7.5bhp at 6000rpm, 60 x 61mm bore and stroke.
£750–850 *BKS*

c1958 Gilera 300 Twin, 304cc, unusual spark plug location at rear of cylinder head.
£1,300–1,500 *NLM*

The later model had a dual seat and Silentium silencers.

1961 Gilera Giubileo 175, 172cc, overhead valve single cylinder, restored, non-original finish.
£1,000–1,200 *IMO*

1942/48 Harley-Davidson Model WLC 45°, 750cc.
£6,500–7,500 *BLM*

Former WD model converted to civilian specification.

1980 Harley-Davidson FLT Tour Guide, 1340cc, every conceivable extra, concours condition.
£8,000–9,000 *HDM*

One of the last machines produced when AMF owned Harley-Davidson.

1949 Harley-Davidson WL45, 750cc, civilian model, side valve V-twin.
£8,500–10,000 *CONQ*

1981 Harley-Davidson FXE Low Rider, 1340cc, Pre-Evo engine, heavily customised and modified. **£7,000–8,200** *HDM*

1973 Hercules W2000 Pre-Series, 294cc, single rotor air-cooled Wankel engine. **£2,000–2,200** *ROW*

A total of 50 Pre-Series machines were built in 1973. Looking much more like the final production batch than the original, 1972 shaft drive prototype machine, the Pre-Series may be distinguished by its yellow tank and Italian-made Grimeca drum front brake.

1966 Honda CB450, 444cc, double overhead camshaft, torsion bar, valve springs, unit construction, concours condition, full restoration. **£3,200–3,700** *PC*

This machine was nicknamed the 'Black Bomber'.

1970 Honda CB750, 736cc, single overhead camshaft, 8 valves, 4 cylinders. **£1,600–1,800** *PC*

Launched in 1969, the CB750 is generally accepted as the first of the modern superbikes.

1972 Honda CL350, 325cc, overhead camshaft twin. **£800–1,000** *PS*

A street scrambler produced for the American market.

1976 Honda CB400F, 408.6cc, standard except for Motad exhaust, sports seat, Hagon rear shocks and black rear mudguard. **£1,000–1,500** *CROW*

1977 Honda CB750F2, 736.5cc, single overhead camshaft, 4 cylinders, standard specifications except for aftermarket exhaust, 5 speed gearbox. **£700–800** *PS*

1978 Honda CB400F2, 408.6cc. **£850–950** *PS*

1959 James Commodore L25, 249cc, AMC engine, single cylinder 2-stroke.
£350–400 *BLM*

1953 Jawa/Ogar, 349cc.
£750–1,000 *CROW*

Ogar-made engine in Jawa plunger frame as first used in Springer model.

1969 Jawa 90 Roadster, 88.7cc, single cylinder air-cooled rotary valve, 2-stroke, 20mm Ikov carburettor, 5-speed gearbox, 9.5bhp, 48 x 49mm bore and stroke.
£300–350 *JCZ*

1973 Kawasaki Z1, 903cc, double overhead camshaft, 4 cylinders.
£3,300–3,600 *PC*

First of the 4 cylinder Kawasaki Superbikes.

1973 Jawa Model 360, 349cc, air-cooled piston port, 2-stroke twin cylinder.
£600–650 *JCZ*

1976 Laverda Jota, 981cc, double overhead camshaft, 3 cylinders, air-cooled, 180° crankshaft.
£3,000–3,500 *GLC*

The Jota arrived in Britain during January 1976 and was the first series production model which could exceed 140mph.

1980 Laverda Formula 500, 498cc.
£3,800–4,200 *IMO*

One of a series of machines built by Laverda for an Italian race series, it is believed around 50 examples were built.

1982 Laverda Jota 180, 981cc, double overhead camshaft, 3 cylinders.
£3,600–3,800 *PC*

Later model with 180°, rather than 360° crankshaft.

1911 Matchless 8hp, JAP V-twin engine.
£10,000–11,500 *VER*

1952 Matchless Spring Twin G9, 498cc, overhead valve vertical twin, separate cast iron cylinders, each with a bore of 66mm having their own separate light alloy cylinder head with cast-in valve seals.
£2,000–2,400 *BLM*

1958 Matchless G3LS, 347cc, overhead valve pre-unit heavyweight single, restored.
£1,900–2,300 *BLM*

1959 Matchless G12, 646cc, overhead valve vertical twin.
£2,200–2,500 *AMOC*

1958 Matchless G9 Clubman, 498cc, stock except period rear carriers.
£1,500–1,800 *PS*

1965 Matchless G80 CS, 498cc, overhead valve heavyweight single cylinder, concours condition.
£2,600–2,800 *AMOC*

1962 Matchless G80 CS, 498cc, overhead valve single cylinder, all-alloy engine, competition model.
£3,500–4,200 *CONQ*

r. **1952 Mondial Sport Volante,** 174cc, overhead camshaft single cylinder, with unit construction, wet-sump and 4 speeds.
£1,900–2,100 *PS*

1948 Moto Guzzi Airone/Astorino, 246cc, overhead valve single cylinder.
£3,500–3,800 *NLM*

1952 Moto Guzzi Falcone, 498.4cc, overhead valve single with horizontal cylinder, restored to concours condition in 1980.
£6,500–7,000 *VMC(P)*

1969 Moto Guzzi Ambassador, 757cc, overhead valve V-twin, shaft drive, 4-speed gearbox, 45bhp at 6000rpm.
£2,500–3,000 *CONQ*

The first of the Guzzi big V-twins was the V7 700 in 1966. The larger V7 Ambassador arrived for 1969.

1979 Moto Guzzi 850 T3, 844cc, overhead valve V-twin, triple disc brakes, alloy rims, very clean, good original condition.
£1,900–2,100 *MoG*

Last of the T3 models, the machine has optional panniers and more comfortable V1000 convert seat.

1983 Moto Guzzi Imola Sports Tourer, 346cc, , V-twin, shaft drive.
£1,500–1,700 *CONQ*

1974 Moto Morino 3½hp, 344cc, 72°, V-twin with Heron head combustion chambers, non-standard front mudguards and silencers.
£1,000–1,200 *MAY*

1983 Moto Morini Kanguro, 344cc, 72°, V-twin, 6-speed gearbox, monoshock rear suspension, early model with drum brakes.
£1,200–1,500 *NLM*

1979 Moto Morini 500, 478cc, 72°, V-twin.
£1,200–1,400 *MORI*

This machine is not entirely original, hence its lower value.

1959 MV Agusta Turismo Rapido Extra, 124cc, overhead valve, 4-speed, full width drum brakes.
£1,200–1,400 *MAY*

1971 MV Agusta 750S, 752.9cc, double overhead camshaft, 4 cylinder.
£14,000–16,000 *KAY*

Coded 214 by the factory only some 500 750S models were built. This one has the rare full fairing and is in pristine condition.

1969 MV Agusta 600 Four, 591cc, double overhead camshaft, 4 cylinders, 5-speed cable-operated disc front brakes.
£12,000–14,000 *KAY*

Debuted at the 1965 Milan Show. Probably the ugliest motorcycle ever built, but as only around 75 were made it is now highly collectible due to its rarity.

c1971 MV Agusta 750S, 752.9cc, double overhead camshaft, 65bhp twin loop frame, sculptured tank, clip-ons, rear sets, humped racing seat, stainless steel mudguards, 4 megaphone silencers.
£12,750–14,500 *BKS*

1977 MV Agusta 750 America, 789cc, double overhead camshaft, 4 cylinders, 20mm carburettors with filter system, original combined black silencers.
£13,000–15,000 *COYS*

Designed for the American market but projected sales never reached expectations due to high price.

1974 MV Agusta 750S, 752.9cc, double overhead camshaft, four cylinders, stored last 5 years, good condition.
£13,000–14,000 *BKS*

This is a later model with disc front brakes, but original Scarab calipers have been replaced by AP Lockheed components.

1914 New Imperial JAP, 250cc, 2-speed, inlet over exhaust, hand change, belt final drive.
£5,000–5,500 *VER*

1937 New Imperial Model 76 De Luxe, 499cc, rare twin port model.
£3,500–3,800 *BLM*

1924 Norton Model TT18, 490cc, overhead valve single cylinder, girder forks, rigid frame, concours condition.
£10,000–11,000 *NOC(C)*

It was the Model 18 with which Norton gained many of its racing successes in the early and mid-1920s, before the introduction of the overhead camshaft models headed by the famous CSI.

1936 Norton Model 40, 348cc, overhead camshaft, 4 speeds, foot change, genuine 26,000 miles recorded.
£7,000–8,000 *NOC*

1937 Norton ES2, 490cc, overhead valve, 4-speed, footchange, girder forks, rigid frame.
£2,000–2,400 *PM*

1949 Norton Model 30 International, 490cc, Manx type petrol tank, drop handlebars, reverse footrests, Brooklands can and alloy wheel trims, good condition.
£5,200–5,700 *BKS*

The Norton International Model 30 has been described as the racer for the road. It is a famous model and is presented in many guises according to the specification required to suit respective owners.

1956 Norton Dominator 88, 497cc, overhead valve vertical twin, Norton gearbox.
£3,000–3,500 *NOC*

The first twins with the featherbed frame were used by the factory in the 1951 ISDT.

1958 Norton Dominator 99 Wideline, 597cc, overhead valve twin cylinder, featherbed frame, roadholder forks and AMC gearbox.
£4,000–4,400 *BLM*

1960 Norton 99 Dominator, 597cc, overhead valve twin cylinder, originally a de-luxe model, restored as standard Model 99.
£2,200–2,600 *NOC*

1960 Norton 99 Dominator, 597cc, overhead valve twin cylinder.
£3,000–3,500 *BLM*

First of the 'slim-line' or 'waisted frames'.

1960 Norton Dominator 88 De Luxe, 497cc, overhead valve vertical twin cylinders, slimline featherbed frame, non-original headlamp and front mudguard.
£2,500–3,000 *BLM*

1962 Norton Jubilee, 249cc.
£650–800 *MAY*

The Jubilee was launched at the 1958 Earl's Court Show.

1964 Norton Atlas, 745cc, 49bhp and 110mph.
£3,800–4,200 *TDC*

When launched on the home market in 1964 the price of the Atlas was £359. It was then the largest capacity vertical twin in the world. This example is standard except for 2LS front brake, alloy rims and recovered seat.

1969 Norton Mercury Café Racer, 646cc, modified to include alloy tank, racing seat, clip-ons, alloy guards, 2LS front brake and Commando silencers.
£3,000–3,500 *BLM*

This stylish café racer was used in a TV advertisement.

1974 Norton Roadster, 745cc, overhead valve, twin cylinders, non-original mudguards, otherwise pristine condition.
£2,500–2,800 *CStC*

1976 Norton Commando Roadster, 828cc, overhead valve, vertical twin cylinders, electric start.
£3,500–4,000 *BLM*

This is one of the limited run Jubilee models.

1952 NSU Fox, 98cc, overhead valve single cylinder, blade forks, swinging arm rear suspension with additional friction dampers.
£700–800 *PC*

This machine is one of a number of smaller NSUs built in Italy during the 1950s.

1952 Panther 75 Rigid, 348cc, overhead valve, 4-speed, telescopic forks, rigid frame.
£1,500–1,800 *BLM*

1956 Panther Model 65, 248cc, overhead valve twin port single, swinging arm, 6.5:1 compression ratio, 60 x 88mm bore and stroke, built 1953–60. **£850–950** *BLM*

Also available with rigid frame (1949–55).

1958 Panther Model 100, 598cc, overhead valve twin port single with sloping cylinder. **£2,800–3,000** *BLM*

The Model 100 originally sported a rigid frame, but swinging arm rear suspension arrived in 1954. The final batch of Deluxe 100s were built in 1963.

1960 Panther Model 100, 598cc, overhead valve twin port single, unrestored. **£1,200–1,500** *AT*

1962 Panther Villiers Model 35 Sports, 249cc, Villiers 2T twin cylinder 2-stroke engine, 50 x 63.5mm bore and stroke. **£650–750** *PM*

1953 Parilla 175 Turismo, 174cc, high camshaft unit construction single, concours condition, fully restored. **£4,000–4,400** *PM*

This model was first produced in 1953.

1963 Panther 120, 649cc, overhead valve twin port single cylinder, 6.5:1 compression rate, 88 x 106mm bore and stroke, concours condition, fully restored. **£3,800–4,000** *WEED*

Built from 1959–66.

1955 Parilla 175, 174cc, high camshaft single cylinder, 4-speed, Dell'Orto UB carburettor, alloy rims, 59.8 x 62mm bore and stroke. **£1,500–1,700** *PC*

1963 Parilla Gran Sports, 247cc, 20bhp at 7000rpm, 68 x 68mm bore and stroke. **£2,700–3,000** *PC*

HARLEY-DAVIDSON *(American 1903–)*

1916 Harley-Davidson 8hp, V-twin, comprehensive restoration.
£10,000–11,000 *BKS*

Harley-Davidson introduced their first V-twin in 1909. However, due to problems with the automatic inlet valve operation, the machine was withdrawn in 1910 pending a redesign. A significantly revised model followed in 1911 which established the pattern of design for subsequent models. Harley were among the first to introduce chain final drive and countershaft gearboxes.

1958 Harley-Davidson FL Duo-Glide, 1200cc, imported from Alabama, USA, work carried out to improve performance, modifications include box section rear swinging arm, rear disc brake, belt primary drive, Mikuni carburettor, late type 'shovel' heads and barrels, Drag specialities seat and pillion pad.
£6,000–7,000 *BKS*

1980 Harley-Davidson Modified Glide, special 1450cc conversion, 5-speed rubber mounted engine.
£8,000–8,500 *HDM*

1974 Harley-Davidson SX175, 174cc, single cylinder piston port 2-stroke, oil pump lubrication, 5-speed, duplex frame.
£300–400 *PC*

Produced in Varese, Italy, at what was formally the Aermacchi plant, the SX175 was an attempt to build a trail bike to compete with the Japanese, notably in the USA. But even though a larger 250 version was also offered the Italian/American challenger never offered a serious threat. Harley-Davidson bought into Aermacchi in 1960, before buying the remainder in 1972. They sold the factory to Cagiva in 1978.

1982 Harley-Davidson FXWG, 1340cc, concours condition, original except for seat, exhaust and handlebars.
£8,000–9,000 *HDM*

HENLEY *(British 1920–29)*

1924 Henley, 349cc, inlet over exhaust single.
£4,000–4,500 *VER*

Don't Forget!

If in doubt please refer to the 'How to Use' section at the beginning of this book.

HERCULES *(German 1904–)*

1975 Hercules W2000 o/i, 294cc, single rotor air-cooled Wankel engine.
£1,800–1,900 *ROW*

The W2000 o/i model was built between October 1974 and November 1975. A total of 639 W2000s were built with a separate oil metering system and became the o/i version. Sold in the UK under the DKW name.

HONDA *(Japanese 1946–)*

1964 Honda CB77, 305cc, overhead camshaft unit construction twin, needing total restoration.
£450–550 *MAY*

1966 Honda C95, 154.6cc, overhead camshaft twin, 49 x 41mm bore and stroke, electric starter.
£900–1,000 *PM*

First produced in 1958 the C95 ran through to the end of 1967.

1965 Honda CS90, 89.5cc, overhead camshaft single with horizontal cylinder.
£1,000–1,500 *BKS*

Also produced as the C200 with pushrod engine.

1966 Honda CB450, 444.9cc, double overhead camshaft twin cylinder, 4-speed, electric starter, concours condition.
£3,600–3,900 *BKS*

The CB450 was launched in April 1965. At the time it was the largest capacity Honda and both the engine and frame included new features along with many common to the existing twins.

1972 Honda CB350/4, 347cc, 32bhp at 9500rpm, 5-speed, disc front brakes.
£400–500 *PS*

1971 Honda CB750 KO, 736cc.
£1,600–1,900 *BKS*

Although introduced in 1969, it was 1970 before any of the Hondas ground-breaking CB750s found their way to British shores, the majority of the early production being absorbed by the American market. This machine is one of the interim KO models that followed the initial CB model onto the market and as such is both rare and desirable.

1978 Honda GL1000 Gold Wing, 999cc, overhead camshaft flat 4, 5-speed, shaft final drive.
£1,900–2,100 *PS*

1980 Honda CB900 F2, 901.8cc, double overhead camshaft, 16 valve, 4 cylinder, 95bhp.
£900–1,100 *PC*

INDIAN *(American 1901–53)*

Scouts, Braves and Chiefs – yes, we are talking Indian, probably the most charismatic of all American bike builders, Harley-Davidson included. The company was founded in 1901 by two former racing cyclists, George M. Hendee and Carl Oscar Hedstrom.

Indian's first production roadster (it also built highly successful racing machines in those pioneering days) was a 4-stroke single with vertical cylinder. With this design and the famous V-twin which made its debut in 1907, Indian soon developed a reputation for sophisticated design and excellent quality that was to stand for many decades.

One of the twins, a 600cc model, was despatched to Britain in the year of its launch and competed in the 1907 ACU Thousand Mile Trial. This event was the forerunner of the world famous ISDT (International Six Days Trial).

With a further eye to exports across the Atlantic, Indian entered no less than four works riders in the 1911 Isle of Man Senior TT. Scoring an impressive 1–2–3, with the help of its newly created 2-speed gearboxes, Indian's reputation in Europe was cemented and in the following year over 20,000 machines were exported.

The Scout 600cc V-twin appeared in late 1919 and was an instant hit. Designed by Charles B. Franklin, Scouts were renowned for their staying power – witness the factory advertising slogan 'You can't wear out an Indian Scout'. This was no idle boast, for a Scout set a new 24-hour road record in 1920, covering 1,114 miles over a closed course in Australia.

The Scout was followed by the 1000cc Chief (1922) and the 1200cc Big Chief a year later. The introduction of the mass-produced car in the USA, combined with import tariffs in the UK by the mid-1920s, followed by the Great Depression in 1929, hit Indian sales hard. However, it was still able to acquire the Ace marque but was eventually taken over in 1930 by E. P. Du Pont.

For the remainder of the 1930s and during WWII Indian soldiered on with profits still proving elusive. In 1949 a cash injection was made by British entrepeneur John Brockhouse. Brockhouse assumed control of Indian, but this failed to halt the company's financial slide and production was terminated in 1953. Since then many have attempted to relaunch the name, including American publisher Floyd Clymer, but without success.

1936 Indian Chief, 1200cc, side valve, V-twin, leaf spring model, rigid frame.
£14,500–16,000 *IMC*

1942 Indian 741B, 500cc, side valve V-twin, ex-military model.
£4,000–4,500 *IMC*

1939 Indian Sport Scout, 600cc, side valve V-twin.
£5,000–5,500 *AT*

1948 Indian Chief, 1200cc, side valve V-twin, blade forks, plunger rear suspension, all correct tin-ware, period panniers.
£14,000–15,000 *IMC*

r. **1951 Indian Brave,** 250cc, side valve single cylinder, rigid frame, telescopic forks.
£1,000–1,500 *IMC*
Made by Brockhouse Engineering, Southport, Lancs, for export to the USA.

Locate the Source
The source of each illustration in Miller's can be found by checking the code letters below each caption with the Key to Illustrations.

r. **1953 Indian Brave,** 248cc, side valve single cylinder, 3-speed, foot change gearbox.
£700–750 *IMC*
British built model sold by Indian dealers from 1951 through to 1953.

l. **1954 Indian Brave,** 250cc, side valve single cylinder, swinging arm frame, telescopic forks, dual seat.
£1,000–1,500 *IMC*
Made by Brockhouse Engineering, Southport, Lancs, for sale in the UK from 1954 to late 1955 before production ceased.

ISH *(Russian 1928–)*

1974 ISH Jupiter, 347cc, piston port, 2-stroke, twin cylinder, original unrestored condition.
£200–300 *PS*

ITOM *(Italian 1948–68)*

1960 Itom Competizione Racer, 49cc.
£1,300–1,600 *S*

These little Italian machines added impetus to the 50cc racing class during the late 1950s by offering clubmen a competitive mount at reasonable cost. The machines all featured a geared primary drive and progressed from a 3-speed gearbox with twist grip operation, via a 4-speed unit with the same operation to a foot-operated unit. Their numerical dominance of the class was finally ended by more powerful production models from other manufacturers.

This is one of the original 3-speed models. Later there was the MkVII with 4 gears, and later still the MkVIII with 4 gears and positive stop change.

JH *(British 1913–21)*

1921 JH2 ½hp TT Model.
£2,000–2,500 *BKS*

James Howard, who had previously worked in the Bradbury factory at Oldham, set up his own motorcycle manufacturing business at Oldham in 1913 building a range of machines powered by proprietary engines (Villiers, JAP and MAG). This machine, formerly owned and restored by VMCC, Past President the late Walter Green, a keen rider and concours exponent, is the only survivor recorded in the VMCC Register of Machines where it is attributed with the date 1919.

It was acquired by Walter Green in 1959, restored in 1960 and has been in storage for many years. Powered by a 2-stroke single cylinder Villiers engine with 2-speed Albion gearbox.

ISO *(Italian 1949–64)*

1957 ISO Moto, 124cc, single cylinder, 2-stroke, good original machine.
£700–800 *AT*

Extremely rare. Made by the same company which produced a range of exclusive cars including the V8 engined Grifo.

JAMES *(British 1902–64)*

1962 James Comet LI, 98cc, Villiers engine, 2 speed gearbox.
£250–350 *AT*

JAWA *(Czechoslovakian 1929–)*

1954 Jawa Model II, 249cc, concours condition.
£900–1,100 *JCZ*

1972 Jawa Model 559, 249cc, air-cooled piston port 2-stroke single cylinder, 4-speed, twin port.
£450–500 *JCZ*

KAWASAKI *(Japanese 1962–)*

Unlike its other Japanese rivals, Kawasaki can rightly claim that motorcycling is only a tiny part of its vast empire because Kawasaki Heavy Industries is one of the world's largest industrial complexes, with interests in shipping, aviation and locomotion, amongst others. Its origins can be traced back to the year 1878, when Shozo Kawasaki founded a shipyard at Tsukiji, Tokyo. In 1881, the Kawasaki Hyogo Shipyard was formed at Higashide-cho, Hyogo, and five years on the two yards were combined to form Kawasaki Shipyard. The company was incorporated in 1896, the first locomotive appeared in 1901, and in 1911 Kawasaki entered the field of marine transportation.

During the WWI, more muscle was added with steel manufacturing facilities. Soon after this, automobile and aviation divisions were established, the latter including production of its own engines. In the quarter of a century to the end of WWII, each of these divisions became prominent in its own sphere as a leader in Japanese industrial might.

When the war ended, Kawasaki, unlike many of its competitors, found its engineering skills in such demand that only one of its many plants was standing idle. This, too, soon found a market niche to keep it busy, producing engine and gearbox assemblies for the rapidly emerging motorcycle industry. One of Kawasaki's customers was Meguro, and it was through this marque that Kawasaki was ultimately to become a bike builder in its own right.

Meguro was taken over by its bigger cousin in 1961 and the following year, 1962, saw the first model to carry a Kawasaki badge, the 125cc B8, a single cylinder 2-stroke. By then Honda, Suzuki and Yamaha were well established in the domestic market and abroad. It is probably true that without its considerable financial and industrial strength, Kawasaki would have been unable to rise to its current position of an equal member of the Japanese Big Four. Along the way it has created some trend-setting machines such as ZI (1973), Z1000 (1977), Z550 (1980), GPZ1100 (1983), GPZ900R (1984), ZXR750 (1989) and ZZR1100 (1990).

Kawasaki has also built a number of interesting and innovative competition motorcycles, from the 1969 world champion 125cc twin (ridden by Dave Simmonds) through to the fearsome 750cc H2-R triple 2-stroke used by the likes of Yvon Du Hamel at Daytona in the early 1970s. There were also the world championship winning 250cc and 350cc KR in-line twin 2-strokes and a hoard of 4-strokes for endurance events, Daytona and Superbike racing.

1968 Kawasaki A1 Samarai, 247cc, disc valve 2-stroke twin cylinder.
£1,800–1,900 *PC*

1969 Kawasaki Mach III, 498cc, 3 cylinder piston port 2-stroke.
£2,400–2,600 *PC*

1975 Kawasaki S1, 246cc.
£460–560 *BKS*

*When introduced into the UK market
this 3 cylinder air-cooled machine set
new standards with excellent
acceleration developed from its 250cc
2-stroke engine and with a top speed
which was staggering for its time. It
continued in production until 1980 but
by this time the machine had been
overshadowed by technical
developments in other directions and
this tended to make it appear more
civilised than the raw edge which was
projected by the earlier versions.*

1977 Kawasaki KH250, 246cc, 3 cylinder 2-stroke engine.
£800–850 *MAY*

Use the Index!

*Because certain items might fit easily into any of
a number of categories, the quickest and surest
method of locating any entry is by reference to the
index at the back of this book. This has been fully
cross referenced for absolute simplicity.*

1977 Kawasaki Z750,
748cc, double overhead
camshaft twin cylinder,
5-speed, disc brakes.
£1,200–1,350 *PC*

r. **1982 Kawasaki Z1000,**
1015cc, double overhead
camshaft 4-cylinder engine.
£1,200–1,400 *MAY*

*The 1000 was basically a
900 with the cylinders
bored out 4mm to 70mm.*

LAVERDA (Italian 1949–)

1976 Laverda 750 SFC Electronica, 744cc,
double overhead camshaft air-cooled twin cylinder.
£10,000–11,000 *COYS*

*The acknowledged flagship of the Laverda line-up,
the 70bhp SFC of 1971 was a thinly disguised
endurance racer aimed at privateer competitors.
For 1975 there were detailed engine changes,
electronic ignition and an oil cooler, with only
130 of these Electronica models being built. Rarer
still – from 549 SFCs built – is the final model
with Laverda thin-web alloy wheels, with
just 30 being produced.*

1980 Laverda Jota, 981cc, double overhead
camshaft 3-cylinders, 5-speed.
£3,600–3,800 *IMO*

*This machine differed from the previous model in
having revised cylinder head, pistons, new rear
shocks, drilled brake discs and new fairing.*

> **Miller's is a price GUIDE
> not a price LIST**

1981 Laverda Jota 1000, 981cc, double overhead camshaft 3 cylinders, 180° crankshaft, 5-speed.
£3,000–4,000 *CONQ*

LEA-FRANCIS (British 1911–26) LEVIS (British 1911–39)

1913 Lea-Francis V-Twin, 498cc, V-twin,
4-stroke, 2-speed, with foot clutch.
£6,000–7,000 *PC*

1930 Levis A3, 349cc, overhead valve,
twin port single cylinder.
£2,500–2,800 *BLM*

MATCHLESS *(British 1901–69, revived 1987)*
The Collier brothers and the first TT race

On the morning of Tuesday, 28 May 1907, 17 singles and eight twins paraded at St John's to have their petrol measured out. Class 1 bikes (singles) were allowed one gallon for every 90 miles, the twins, one for every 75. They had to cover ten laps of the 15.8 mile course and machines started in pairs every minute. Pedalling gear was permitted!

Among these original entries for the first ever Isle of Man motorcycle TT (Tourist Trophy) were Harry Collier Junior and Charlie Collier, each riding a 3½hp overhead valve Matchless single.

Harry Collier Senior and his two sons can rightly be counted amongst the true pioneers of the British motorcycle industry. They had begun activities in London back in 1901 using De Dion and MMC engines, having constructed an experimental Matchless two years earlier in 1899.

Although Norton mounted Rem Fowler riding a Peugeot-engined V-twin won the twin cylinder class, it was largely the Collier brothers who dominated this initial TT series, with Charlie winning the single cylinder class in 4 hours 8 minutes and 8.2 seconds, at an average speed of 38.33mph, despite broken forks, while his brother set the fastest lap of the singles class with a time of 23 minutes 5⅗ seconds (41.81mph). In fact it would have been a Matchless 1–2 but for Harry Junior's exhaust valve breaking on lap 9, smashing the piston and putting him out of the running.

The Matchless machines ridden by the Collier brothers in this first Isle of Man motorcycle Tourist Trophy were powered by London-built JAP (James Alfred Prestwich) engines with a capacity of 432cc and featuring overhead valves operated by pushrods. Both of the specially prepared power units had an 85mm bore and 76mm stroke – and this in an age when it was almost universal to have long-stroke dimensions.

1934 Matchless Model X, 990cc, side valve V-twin.
£5,000–6,000 *VER*

1941 Matchless G3L Rigid, 347cc, overhead valve single port, 4-speed, footchange, telescopic forks.
£1,200–1,300 *BLM*

1937 Matchless Model 37/X, 990cc.
£6,000–6,500 *BKS*

1937 saw the introduction of a considerably revised 990cc side valve, V-twin Model X costing £72 10s 0d in solo form with a full lighting set when new. The entensively redesigned engine incorporated Ricardo type cylinder heads and repositioned exhaust ports to aid both performance and cooling, and shared a new shorter frame with a 4-speed Burman gearbox. The parts were stoved black to Matchless's usual impeccable standard and were crowned with a chromium-plated tank with black panels and gold lining featuring a tank top instrument panel, resulting in one of the most handsome machines of its era.

1950 Matchless G80, 498cc, overhead valve, iron head and barrel, 4-speed footchange gearbox, AMC Teledraulic forks, rigid frame.
£1,800–2,000 *AT*

1953 Matchless G80, 498cc, overhead valve single cylinder, AMC Teledraulic forks and 'jampot' rear suspension units.
£2,000–2,250 *BLM*

1953 Matchless Model G9, 498cc, overhead valve vertical twin cylinder, spring frame, short dumpy megaphone silencers, single-sided brake drums, restored condition.
£2,000–2,200 *AT*

1954 Matchless G3LS, 347cc.
£2,300–2,600 *BKS*

This G3LS is a typical, medium capacity stalwart from the mid-1950s, which was well engineered, solid and dependable. It was tremendously economical to use and a safe motorcycle to ride which, combined with its reliability and economy, made it a popular machine for the everyday motorcyclist. It was powered by a 347cc single cylinder overhead valve engine and shared similar cycle parts to the 498cc model of the range.

1954 Matchless G3LS, 347cc, overhead valve, full width front brake.
£1,500–1,750 *AT*

1957 Matchless G3LS, 348cc, overhead valve single cylinder.
£1,800–1,900 *PC*

The G3LS epitomises the best aspects of the traditional heavyweight British single – robustness with a reasonable price tag – both when new and now. As far as the engine was concerned it had very few changes in its long career which spanned the late 1930s until the mid-1960s.

l. **1965 Matchless G12,** 646cc, overhead valve vertical twin cylinder, non-standard seat and mudguards, earlier silencers.
£1,500–1,700 *MAY*

1958 Matchless G3LS, 350cc, overhead valve air-cooled engine, vertical single cylinder, engine overhauled, good original condition.
£1,400–1,600 *BKS*

The Matchless G3LS was manufactured by AMC at Plumstead from 1949 to 1963 and actually changed little during its production run so successful was its original basic design.

McKENZIE *(British 1921–25)*

1925 McKenzie, 170cc.
£800–1,000 *VER*

MOTOBI *(Italian 1951–76)*

1964 Motobi 200 Sprite, 199cc, overhead valve horizontal single cylinder.
£1,400–1,800 *PC*

One of the 6 Benelli brothers, Guiseppe, left the company in 1949 to set up the rival Motobi marque. A characteristic was the horizontal cylinder and egg-shaped crankcase.

MOTO GUZZI *(Italian 1921–)*

The winged eagle, Moto Guzzi's emblem, is the result of a fatal flying accident sustained by one of a trio of men whose dream it was to create their own motorcycle. Giorgio Parodi, Giovanni Ravelli and Carlo Guzzi met during WWI during service with the Italian air-arm. A few short days after the end of hostilities Ravelli was killed while testing his biplane.

Despite this setback, Parodi and Guzzi realised their ambition with financial help from Parodi's father, a wealthy shipping magnate from the port of Genoa. From only ten employees in 1921, including the two partners, Moto Guzzi rose to become Italy's largest and most famous factory employing hundreds.

Right from the start it took a great interest in racing and until its withdrawal from the sport at the end of 1957, it favoured a horizontal single cylinder engine layout, and with its basic design Guzzi machines and riders won ten TTs and eight World Championships.

Although the Mandello del Lario factory achieved numerous Continental victories in its early days, it was not until 1935, when Stanley Woods won both the Lightweight and Senior TTs, that Guzzi's efforts were crowned with truly international success. Other notable pre-war victories came in the 1937 Lightweight TT and the epic defeat of the mighty DKWs in the 1939 250cc German Grand Prix.

During the war Guzzi turned its hand to building military motorcycles, a trend it was to continue when peace finally came, together with police bikes for customers around the world.

Remaining faithful to its horizontal single cylinder racer didn't stop Guzzi designing other formats for track use, including V-twin, across-the-frame 3-cylinders, in-line 4 cylinders and even a V8!

Then in the 1960s came the financial decline that was to lead ultimately to takeover by the Argentinian industrialist De Tomaso in 1972. In the De Tomaso era the shaft drive V7 (V-twin 700cc) military/police bike first seen in 1965 was developed by Lino Tonti into a range of touring and sports bikes, including the V7 Sport (1972), 850T3 (1975) and 850 Le Mans (1976).

In 1994 the management of the company was taken over by Finprogetti. In 1995 Guzzi doubled its sales and was able to balance its books once again. In 1997 it was employing 350 personnel and looked set to launch several new models before the turn of the century.

1956 Moto Guzzi Airone Sport,
246cc, speedo, Dell'Orto SS carburettor, completely original, unrestored.
£2,000–2,350 *NLM*

r. **1962 Moto Guzzi Lodola GT,**
235cc, overhead valve, concours condition.
£2,100–2,300 *IMO*

The original Lodola (Carlo Guzzi's last design) was a 175 with overhead camshaft which made its debut in 1956. The pushrod model with larger capacity debuted in 1960.

1963 Moto Guzzi Galletto Elettrico, 192cc,
overhead valve, 4 speed, leading link front suspension.
£1,000–1,200 *MoG*
The final version of the 'half motorcycle / half scooter'
was built from 1961–66, featuring many changes
including an electric start, more power, higher
compression ratio, final drive gearing and totally
revised bodywork.

1969 Moto Guzzi Stornello Sport America,
123cc, overhead valve unit construction, 4-speed,
17in wheels.
£800–900 *MoG*

l. **1974 Moto Guzzi 750S,** 748cc.
£1,600–1,800 *BKS*

An engine design which originated in the early
post-war years to fulfil the Italian military's need
for a lightweight jeep-type vehicle, Moto Guzzi's
venerable 90° V-twin is still around today powering
the latest generation of superbikes from Mandello
del Lario. The first motorcycle to make use of this
remarkable engine, the 703cc V7, appeared in the
late 1960s. Enlargement to 757cc soon followed, but
the first sports model, the V7S of 1971, was of 748cc
capacity. The V7S featured a new frame for
improved handling, alternator electrics and an
increase in power which boosted top speed to
120mph. A 5-speed gearbox was standard equipment,
and the brakes were large diameter drums, the front
a double-sided twin leading shoe unit.

1975 Moto Guzzi 750 S3, 748cc,
overhead valve, V-twin, shaft final drive.
£3,000–3,500 *CONQ*

The 750S3 was the last of the 750 sporting Guzzi
series of the early 1970s. It utilised many of the
larger 850 T3's components including the triple
disc, linked brake system.

r. **1977 Moto Guzzi 850 T3 California,**
844cc, overhead valve, V-twin, shaft drive,
5-speed, screen, panniers, footboards,
crashbars, peaked headlamp rim.
£2,800–3,000 *MoG*

1978 Moto Guzzi 350 GTS, 345.5cc, single overhead camshaft, chain driven, across-the-frame, air-cooled, 4 cylinders, 5-speed, 4,000 miles from new, 38bhp at 9500rpm.
£900–1,000 *MAY*

Locate the Source

The source of each illustration in Miller's can be found by checking the code letters below each caption with the Key to Illustrations.

l. **1979 Moto Guzzi 400 GTS,** 397cc, single overhead camshaft four, 40bhp at 9500rpm, maximum speed 102mph.
£1,600–1,800 *S*

Based on the smaller 350GTS Four, the 400 version was achieved by lengthening the stroke, rather than the bore, from 44 to 50.6mm, providing almost square 50 x 50.6mm dimensions.

1982 Moto Guzzi V35 Imola, 346cc, overhead valve, V-twin, triple disc brakes, cast alloy wheels.
£1,400–1,500 *MAY*

The Imola was the sports version of the standard V35 which was launched in 1977. The first Imolas appeared in 1979 and ran through to 1983.

MOTO MORINI *(Italian 1937–)*

1953 Moto Morini 125 Turismo, 123cc, piston port
2-stroke single cylinder, to original specification.
£1,000–1,200 *PC*

This machine was the Italian version of the Bantam.

1961 Moto Morini Tresette Sprint 175, 174cc,
overhead valve, wet sump lubrication, 4-speed,
alloy rims, Silentium silencer.
£2,350–2,650 *NLM*

1974 Moto Morini 125 Turismo, 124cc,
overhead valve unit construction engine.
£700–800 *MORI*

1974 Moto Morini 3½ Sport, 344cc.
£2,800–3,000 *NLM*

*This was largely seen as the definitive Morini V-twin, the wire wheel 3½ Sport with double drum front
brake, alloy rims, round bum-stop seat, clip-ons and stainless steel mudguards.*

1976 Moto Morini Valentini 460, 460cc.
£2,800–3,000 *IMO*

In Italy, the Morini tuner Valentini made quite an impact during the late 1970s and early 1980s in Formula 3 racing. He also offered a range of tuning/customising goodies for road riders, and even went as far as producing a small number of sporting roadsters in either 344cc or big bore 460cc form.

l. **1978 Moto Morini 250T,** 239cc.
£1,200–1,500 *MORI*

The 250 single was originally intended for use by municipal or government departments, following a trend set by Moto Guzzi. A few machines were subsequently sold for civilian use, of which this is one example.

1976 Moto Morini 3½ Sport Valentini, 344cc.
£5,500–6,000 *NLM*

This unique machine was constructed using virtually every Valentini accessory, including frame mods, tuned engine and several other features. Valentini was to Morini what Cooper was to Mini or Abarth to Fiat.

1978 Moto Morini 250T, 239cc, rubber-mounted engine, basically half a 500 V-twin.
£1,200–1,500 *NLM*

1980 Moto Morini 3½ Sport, 344cc, overhead valve V-twin, gold cast wheels, black exhaust, red frame, concours condition.
£2,500–2,700 *PC*

1981 Moto Morini 500 Sport, 478.6cc, non-standard silencers.
£1,600–1,800 *MORI*

1981 Moto Morini 500, 478cc, 72°, V-twin engine, 5-speed, triple disc brakes, concours condition.
£2,400–2,600 *PC*

The original 500 Morini in pre-production form was first shown at the Milan Show in November 1975. However, production was slow in getting under way and only small numbers were built in 1977–78. In 1979 the 500 was restyled as shown here. Later still from the beginning of 1982 a 6-speed gearbox was specified.

> **Miller's is a price GUIDE not a price LIST**

1981 Moto Morini 250 2C, 239cc, 72° V-twin, 59 x 43.8mm bore and stroke, maximum 87mph.
£1,200–1,400 *NLM*

Morini's smallest V-twin. Its sales were limited by a relatively high price, even though, compared with the larger vees, there were cost cutting features such as painted mudguards and plastic chainguard.

1982 Moto Morini 500 Camel, 478.6cc.
£1,700–1,800 *MORI*

1983 Moto Morini 500 SE-V, 478.6cc, 6-speed gearbox, clip-ons, chrome exhaust, sports seat, concours condition.
£2,400–2,600 *PC*

1983 Moto Morini 500, 478.6cc, 6-speed, touring model, conventional handlebars, non-standard rear carrier.
£1,900–2,000 *PC*

l. **1983 Moto Morini 250 2C,** 239cc.
£1,300–1,500 *MORI*

The smallest Morini V-twin used the basic frame parts from the company's 250 single to keep down costs, but it was still an expensive bike to buy when new.

1984 Moto Kanguro X3, 346cc.
£1,500–2,000 *NLM*

This is a later model with disc front and rear brakes, styling changes, standard Paris-Dakar type tank.

1988 Moto Morini Dart, 344cc, low mileage, excellent condition.
£2,500–3,000 *NLM*

The last Morini sportster, the 350 Dart was a clever mix of bike cultures – combining a Cagiva Freccia 125 chassis with a Morini V-twin engine. Also built in 400cc guise.

MV AGUSTA *(Italian 1945–78)*

1959 MV Agusta Turismo Rapido Extra,
124cc, overhead valve.
£400–500 *MAY*

*In need of restoration, with original leg shields,
tatty, but complete.*

1957 MV Agusta Turismo Rapido, 124cc,
overhead valve, 4-speed.
£600–750 *PC*

*Typical of the many small commuter ultra-lightweight
motorcycles built by MV Agusta during the 1950s.*

> **Miller's is a price GUIDE
> not a price LIST**

1972 MV Agusta 350B, 349cc.
£1,950–2,150 *BKS*

*Better known for their racing and road-going multi-cylinder machines, MV Agusta also built a range of
single and twin cylinder sports bikes during the 1960s and 1970s. Intermittently available in Britain
throughout this period, their high price meant that they were never top sellers. This MV Agusta 350 has
a twin cylinder overhead valve engine breathing through 2 Dell'Orto carburettors. Of unit construction, the
motor features gear primary drive to a 5-speed transmission. Claimed maximum power was 32bhp and the
top speed in excess of 90mph.*

r. **1971 MV Agusta
750GT,** 752.9cc,
double overhead
camshaft, 4 cylinders.
£14,000–18,000 *KAY*

*Only some 135
examples of the Model
214 Strada were built.
They are now virtually
extinct as most have
been converted to hotter
750S specification.*

1973 MV Agusta 750S, 749cc, double overhead camshaft four, concours condition.
£17,000–19,000 *PC*

This machine was imported into Denmark during 1973 by the Danish MV Agusta concessionaire for his own use. The only 4 cylinder MV ever officially imported into that country.

1974 MV Agusta Sport Model 214, 752.9cc, double overhead four camshaft.
£15,000–17,000 *KAY*

The final batch of 750S models came with Scarab-made twin front disc brakes. This also has factory-built fairing.

1978 MV Agusta Magni, 867cc.
£20,000–25,000 *KAY*

Built after the works had closed by Arturo Magni (ex-factory race mechanic and later team manager) some 80 machines using either 832 or 867cc engines were constructed. Price in 1978 was between £10,000–15,000 depending upon exact specification. The definitive MV four and also the best looking, best handling and fastest.

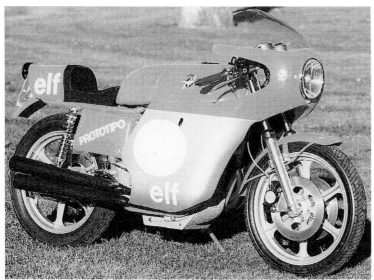

l. **c1978 MV Agusta Agostini Replica,** 789cc.
£12,700–14,000 *BKS*

This example of MV Agusta's legendary 4 cylinder model first came to the attention of enthusiasts towards the end of the 1970s purporting to be an ex-Agostini works racer. It now seems most likely that it was built in Britain utilising components from the 'America' model and one-off items to produce a machine that echoed the looks of the factory's Formula 750 racer that competed at Imola in 1972 in Agostini's hands. It can be described as an Agostini Replica. Restored by leading MV specialist, David Kay, finished in MV's traditional red and silver livery with stainless steel fasteners.

NER-A-CAR *(American/British 1921–26)*

1924 Ner-A-Car 2¼hp, 285cc, 2-stroke with Simplex engine, good original condition.
£3,000–3,250 *AT*

NEW HUDSON *(British 1909–57)*

l. **1932 New Hudson Twin Port,** 350cc,
overhead valve, twin port single, hand
change gearbox, needs restoration.
£1,600–1,800 *BKS*

*Based at Birmingham the New Hudson
factory at one time was a prolific
producer of motorcycles. In 1930 they
revealed their new generation of machines
including the top of the range sports
tuned Bronze Wing and their future
seemed secure. However, the Depression
arrived and with much money spent on
the new line-up by 1933 they were forced
to cease production of motorcyles.*

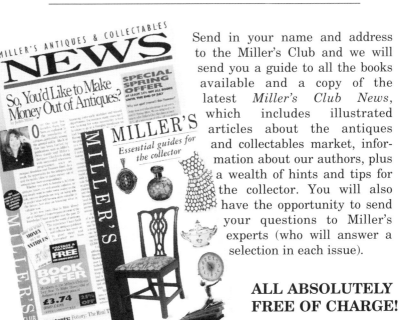

NEW IMPERIAL *(British 1910–39)*

1921 New Imperial Model 7, 998cc, inlet over exhaust, belt final drive, hand gear change.
£9,500–10,000 *BKS*

Manufactured in Hack Street, Birmingham, from about 1900 under the trade name of New Imperial Cycles, a range of machines of all capacities was promoted right up until 1939 when unfortunately production ceased. The large capacity V-twin was fitted with the legendary side valve JAP engine and independent gearbox. The design was basically the same as many similar, large capacity machines of the era but because the factory was relatively small these machines were not made in any great numbers.

1925 New Imperial SV, 349cc, side valve single cylinder.
£2,000–2,300 *PM*

1935 New Imperial Model 30, 247cc, overhead valve single, sloping cylinder, unit construction engine.
£1,900–2,100 *PS*

1936 New Imperial Clubman, 349cc, overhead valve single, girder forks, rigid frame.
£2,700–3,000 *PS*

NORMAN *(British 1937–61)*

Prices
The price ranges given reflect the average price a purchaser should pay for a similar motorcycle. Condition, rarity of model, pedigree, restoration and many other factors must be taken into account when assessing values.

l. **1954 Norman B2S,** 197cc.
£500–700 *PS*

Made in Ashford, Kent, Norman produced a range of Villiers-engined machines during the immediate post-war days, until the mid-1960s. The B2S was produced from 1952 until 1958, and employed a single cylinder Villiers 6E engine with 3-speed gearbox.

NORTON *(British 1902–)*
Norton built more military 16H's than any other model

As a war machine, the motorcycle replaced the horse as an important means of communication, while in sidecar vogue it established itself as a functional and highly mobile light assault vehicle or transporter.

In WWI the British with their Douglas 350s, Triumph 550s, Rudge Multis and P&Ms led the way, but were joined, following America's entry into the conflict in 1917, by a host of Harley-Davidsons, Indians and Excelsiors. Other early military motorcycles included FN (Belgium), NSU (Germany) and Puch (Austro-Hungary).

During the inter-war period of the 1920s and 1930s virtually every European nation designed and built its own military motorcycles in an amazing array of engine types and capacities. From then Czechoslovakia Republic came the Walter 750 V-twin (1923), BD500 (1926), Praga 449cc overhead camshaft single (1928), Jawa 346cc SV (1934), CZ 175 2-stroke (1935) and Jawa 175 2-stroke (1937). Germany produced the Victoria KR overhead valve twin (1925), BMW R52 and R62 (both 1928), R4 398cc overhead valve single (1932), Zündapp K500/800 (1934), BMW R61 and R71 (1938), DKW RT125 and NZ 350 (1938) and TWN B350 (1938).

France contributed the René Gillet G&H (1928), Peugeot P107 (1930) and P53 (1934), Motobecane B1V2 and S5C (1934), Monet Goyon L5A1 (1935) and Gnome et Rhone 721cc overhead valve and 804 single valve horizontal twins (1938). British efforts included the Douglas Military 350 (1929), Triumph CSD (1929), BSA Military Model (1933) and in 1938 the BSA B21, M20, M21 and G14. Mussolini's Italy saw the Moto Guzzi GT (1928), GT17 (1932), GTV (1935), Bianchi 496cc single valve single (1936), Benelli Model 500 (1939) and Moto Guzzi Alce (1939).

There were also specialised military bikes built in Poland, Belgium, the Soviet Union, Sweden, Switzerland and Denmark, not to mention the USA and Japan.

When Germany marched into Poland on 1 September 1939 many countries in Europe had been on almost a war footing for several months since the Munich Crisis of a year earlier. Thanks to an inspired move, Norton had foregone its usual challenge for road racing honours during the 1939 season, concentrating instead on military contracts thanks to the persistence of its managing director, Gilbert Smith.

The machine Norton was building was the 490cc side valve Model 16H single. This was basically a 1937 civilian model with the military conversion consisting of little more than a crankcase shield, a pillion seat or rear carrier rack, a pair of canvas pannier bags, provision for masked lighting, and an overall coat of khaki paint. The Birmingham Bracebridge Street factory also built the very similar Big Four with larger 634cc capacity. Some 100,000 16H's alone were built for wartime service showing how Smith's foresight was to pay dividends.

So Norton's most popular bike was not a Sportster, in fact not even a civilian model, but instead a military side valve single!

1925 Norton 16H, 490cc, side valve single cylinder.
£5,500–5,750 *VER*

Equipped with drum front brake, Norton claimed the 16H was the fastest side valve machine on the market. The price of £72 was something like 6 months' wages for a working man during the mid-1920s.

1928 Norton Model 18, 490cc, overhead valve,
3-speed Sturmey-Archer gearbox and mechanical
oil pump, Druid front forks, largely original.
£7,000–7,500 *NOC(C)*

r. **1931 Norton CSI,** 490cc,
overhead camshaft single.
£4,000–4,500 *PS*

*The CSI production model was a
replica roadster of Alex Bennett's
1927 TT winning machine.*

l. **1935 Norton ES2,** 490cc,
overhead valve single cylinder.
£2,500–2,700 *BKS*

*Basically the layout of the ES2 engine
remained unchanged for 40 years, it was
an economical, slow revving workhorse
which adhered itself to many because of
its renowned reliability and economy in
use. This was of paramount importance
during the 1930s and the model
continued to be built at Bracebridge
Street during the whole period that
Norton produced motorcycles there.*

1946 Norton Model 18, 490cc, overhead valve, telescopic forks, pillion pad, two owners,
with original toolkit, tyre pump and Lucas battery.
£2,200–2,500 *PS*

1948 Norton Model 30 International, 490cc, overhead camshaft, single cylinder, 4-speed, foot change, telescopic forks, plunger frame, Brooklands can silencer.
£5,000–6,000 *VER*

Don't Forget!
If in doubt please refer to the 'How to Use' section at the beginning of this book.

1948 Norton Model 18, 490cc, overhead valve single cylinder, original period trim.
£2,700–3,200 *BLM*

l. **1950 Norton Model 7,** 497cc, overhead valve, vertical trim.
£2,700–3,000 *VER*

The first of the twin cylinder Nortons of the post-war era, the Model 7 was designed by Bert Hopwood and announced in November 1948.

1952 Norton ES2, 490cc, overhead valve single, iron head and barrel, 4-speed, foot change, tele plunger (garden gate) model with single saddle.
£2,000–2,200 *AT*

1953 Norton ES2, 490cc, overhead valve single cylinder, 79 x 100mm, 21bhp at 5300rpm.
£2,300–2,600 *PC*

Changes to the ES2 for 1953 saw a swinging arm frame based on the old-type brazed lug construction with single top and down tubes, not the Featherbed racing-derived type. At the same time a smaller exhaust pipe and pear-shaped silencer were fitted, whilst the gearing was altered with the fitment of a 43 tooth rear wheel sprocket.

1954 Norton ES2, 490cc, overhead valve wideline Featherbed frame, with café racer modifications including clip-ons, rear sets, racing seat, alloy rims and central oil tank.
£2,900–3,100 *NOC(C)*

r. **1954 Norton Big 4,** 596cc, single valve.
£2,100–2,300 *BKS*

This Norton big single is powered by a 596cc side valve single port engine and was in production from before the 1920s into the 1950s. It was the big 4-stroke workhorse of the Norton range with ample pulling power, and was a solid, reliable and economical machine to run.

1955 Norton Model 30 International, 490cc, overhead camshaft.
£9,000–10,000 *TDC*

The last of the famous international models sported wideline Featherbed frames. This machine has not only been raced in the Manx GP, but has also had a full rebuild to concours condition.

1957 Norton ES2, 490cc, overhead valve, telescopic forks and swinging arm frame.
£2,000–2,200 *AT*

1958 Norton Model 50, 348cc, overhead valve single cylinder.
£2,000–2,500 *BLM*
This model was built in the final year before both the Model 50 and ES2 singles went over to the Featherbed frame which was already used for the twin cylinder models.

1959 Norton Model 50, 348cc, overhead valve single cylinder, engine overhauled, original gearbox, stainless fasteners, converted to 3-phase alternator, Tomaselli levers, Marzochi shock absorbers and Cibie headlamp.
£2,000–2,400 *NOC*

This bike has been in everyday use since 1969. Used for holidays and rallies both in the UK and on the Continent including France, Czech Republic and Italy.

1959 Norton Model 50, 349cc, overhead valve single, wideline Featherbed frame, roadholder forks, coil ignition, AMC gearbox, Forest Green, 28,000 miles, two owners only, concours condition.
£2,900–3,100 *PC*

> **Make the most of Miller's**
>
> *Condition is absolutely vital when assessing the value of a motorcycle. Top class bikes on the whole appreciate much more than less perfect examples. Rare, desirable bikes may command higher prices even when in need of restoration.*

1961 Norton Navigator, 348cc.
£860–960 *BKS*

In 1962 the announcement came that Norton was to leave Bracebridge Street. This machine is, therefore, from the last year of production from the famous factory. The Navigator and its smaller companion the 250cc Jubilee was introduced in 1958. The model has a unit construction engine with slightly inclined cylinders and overhead valves with gear driven camshafts and an alternator. The machine was given a streamlined appearance, a two colour finish and a newly designed long tank badge.

1962 Norton Navigator, 348cc, overhead valve twin cylinder, roadholder forks, factory fitted side stand, flat bars and enclosed rear chain case, Boyer electronic ignition.
£800–1,200 *NOC*

Has completed several tours and rallies including Jersey, Isle of Man, plus trips all over England.

1962 Norton 650SS, 646cc, overhead valve twin cylinder, modifications include modern tyres, alloy rims, electronic ignition, indicators.
£2,500–3,000 *NOC*

This machine has been used for commuting, as a family sidecar outfit, was raced in the Thruxton 500 mile Endurance Race and was a café racer style for a short period.

1972 Norton Commando Roadster 750, 745cc, overhead valve twin, Isolastic frame.
£2,700–3,000 *BLM*

The first Commando models went on sale in April 1968 and quickly became the top-selling British bike and was voted Motorcycle News *'Machine of the Year', on more than one occasion.*

1974 Norton Commando Interstate, 828cc.
£2,500–2,900 *BKS*

Norton unveiled the twin cylinder 750cc Commando in 1967 using the Atlas engine in the revolutionary Isolastic frame. The new Isolastic mounting prevented both engine and road vibration being transmitted to the rider, resulting in an exceptionally smooth ride for a large twin. The engine size was later increased to 828cc without any loss of smoothness.
This 1974 828cc Interstate is one of 20 supplied new to the Nigerian Police Force and was rescued by an Englishman who returned it to the UK and restored it.

1966 Norton Atlas, 745cc.
£2,300–2,500 *BKS*

Norton's 500 twin appeared in the racing singles' Featherbed frame in November 1951. Initially for export only, the Dominator Model 88 was the first production Norton to feature the lightweight race-proven chassis. Norton's next twin was a 600, a full-sized 650 not appearing until the launch of the US market Manxman in 1960. Available to European customers the following year, the Dominator 650 was built in standard, de luxe, and SS variations, all of which plus the 500SS featured a new cylinder head with downdraught inlet ports. A 750 model of the Atlas appeared soon after. Initially for export only, the Atlas did not reach the home market until 1964.

1974 Norton JPS 850, 828cc, overhead valve twin, essentially an Interstate with special bodywork, concours condition, full restoration.
£3,700–4,000 *NOC(C)*

In the mid-1970s Norton built a small series of the JPS models to cash in on the factory racing team. These are now rare and are highly prized by collectors.

1974 Norton 850 Interstate MkII,
828cc, overhead valve twin.
£2,200–2,500 *CStC*

Interstates had larger fuel tanks than Roadsters.

1975 Norton Commando Roadster,
828cc, overhead valve vertical twin.
£3,500–4,000 *BLM*

1975 Norton Commando MkIII, 828cc,
overhead valve twin cylinder, modifications
include Boyer electronic ignition, Dymag
alloy wheels, King and Queen seat,
rear luggage carrier, touring fairing,
direction indicators.
£2,500–2,900 *NOC*

*This machine was taken to Australia
twice where it successfuly completed
2 Marathon Tours.*

1975 Norton Commando Interstate MkII, 828cc.
£3,500–4,000 *BLM*

*The Interstate was launched in March 1973 and the engine
enlarged. The MkIII was launched in April 1975 with an
American Prestolite electric start and left-hand gear
change. This example is one of the final MkIIs with right-
hand change. Another addition on the MkIII was disc,
instead of drum rear brake.*

1987 Norton Rotary Classic, 588cc, twin rotor air-cooled Wankel engine.
£4,500–6,000 *ROW*

*A total of 101 Classics were manufactured during 1987 and 1988. Potential buyers should be aware that
several ex-Police and ex-RAF Interpol 2 machines have been converted into Classic Replicas. Ensure that
the frame numbers are between LE–001 and LE–101. (LE – Limited Edition).*

NSU *(German 1901–67)*

One of the pioneers of the German motorcycle industry was NSU (Neckarsulmer Strickwaren Union), named after the company's location at Neckarsulm, where the rivers Neckar and Ulm join. It developed first by producing sewing machines in 1880, bicycles from 1887, while the first motorcycle was built in 1901; five years later NSU introduced its first car to the public.

The 1901 NSU was equipped with an engine made by the Swiss Zedal Company. This was a single cylinder, 234cc 4-stroke. Basically it was a motorised bicycle, with unsprung frame, the engine being driven by a leather belt to the rear wheel. Soon NSU switched to engines of its own construction. By the end of WWI, NSU were building machines with V-twin engines with capacities ranging from 496 to 996cc, mounted in steel tubular frames.

The Neckarsulm factory pioneered 'production line' techniques during 1929. That same year also saw the appointment of the famous English designer Walter Moore (who had created the first overhead camshaft Norton in 1927) and the start of the Depression that nearly killed off NSU, which survived only by the skin of its corporate teeth.

From 1932 onwards the rebirth began, and in 1939 the company had its best year yet,

when almost 63,000 motorcycles were built. The same year also saw the technically advanced, supercharged 345cc double overhead camshaft vertical twin racer, which for speed was unsurpassed in its day.

The war saw NSU involved in many different fields, even building the *Kattenkrad* (a small, tracked, personnel carrier – half motorcycle, half truck). With the end of hostilities in 1945, NSU, unlike many of its great rivals, found itself in the Western sector of Germany, enabling the company to begin building motorcycles again by 1948.

Its most famous post-war roadsters were the 247cc overhead camshaft Max and its moped, the 49cc Quickly, the latter being built in vast quantities – an amazing 1.1 million of all versions!

NSU was also prominent in motorcycle sport during the 1950s, winning a trio of successive 250cc world road racing titles (1953–55) and two 125cc crowns (1953 and 1954), plus countless gold medals in long distance trials and several world speed records for both solos and sidecars.

By the time NSU was swallowed up by the Volkswagen group in 1969 it had already quit the motorcycle scene, leaving BMW as the only major German marque.

c1916 NSU Sprung Frame, 596cc, inlet over exhaust, V-twin.
£10,500–12,000 *AtMC*

NSU built a series of V-twins with engine capacities of 496, 596, 746 and 996cc.

r. **1956 NSU Superfox,** 123cc, overhead valve single, cylinder, 4-speed, foot change, 8.8bhp at 6500rpm, 7.8:1 compression ratio, 19in wheels, 10.8 litre tank, 60mph.
£1,200–1,500 *PS*

The Superfox replaced the earlier Fox models.

1960 NSU Supermax, 247cc.
£2,600–2,900 *PC*

Developed from the earlier Max and Special Max models, the Supermax was the final development of the very unorthodox Ultramax valve gear system designed by Albert Roder. The drive to the overhead valve gear was by long connecting rods housed in a tunnel cast on the left of the cylinder barrel. At their ends, these rods carried eye encircling counter-balanced eccentric discs connected to the half-time pinion and overhead camshaft. As the engine revolved, so the eccentrics imparted a reciprocating motion which was transferred to the valve gear. Hairpin valve springs were used and the entire mechanism was enclosed.

1957 NSU Sportmax, 247cc, overhead camshaft, 5-speed, alloy tank, Norton front brake.
£3,800–4,100 *PC*

OK-SUPREME *(British 1899–39)*

1927 OK-Supreme Model G28, 249cc, overhead valve single, hand change, chain final drive.
£6,000–7,000 *VER*

OMEGA *(British 1919–27)*

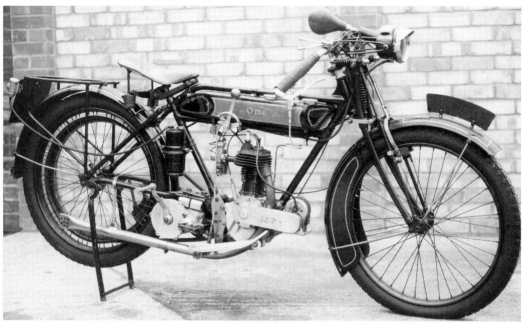

c1919 Omega, 248cc, JAP inlet over exhaust single cylinder engine.
£3,900–4,100 *AtMC*

PANTHER (P&M)
(British 1900–66)

1917 P&M Panther 3½hp, 498cc, inlet over exhaust single with sloping cylinder, good, sound older restoration.
£6,000–7,000 *AT*

After extensive trials P&M were selected to supply their 3½hp model as the standard equipment to the newly formed Royal Flying Corps in 1914.

1937 Panther 100 Redwing Sloper, 598cc, overhead valve long stroke twin port single, 87 x 100mm.
£3,000–3,500 *BLM*

r. **1964 Panther Model 120,** 649cc, overhead valve twin port single, mechanically sound.
£1,500–1,800 *AT*

PARILLA *(Italian 1946–67)*

1956 Parilla 175GT, 174cc, high camshaft single cylinder, 9bhp at 6800rpm, 65mph.
£2,000–2,200 *PC*

1961 Parilla 175 Sport, 174cc, high camshaft single, 4-speed, unit construction, full width hubs, alloy rims, concours condition, fully restored.
£2,900–3,100 *PC*

15bhp at 7500rpm, the even more highly tuned Derivato MSDS was a Formula 3 racer with a maximum speed of over 90mph.

PEUGEOT *(French 1899–)*

Peugeot is one of the famous names in the automobile world, but it has also played an important role in the development of the motorcycle.

In 1810 Jean Frédéric and Jean Pierre Peugeot opened a small foundry, that was instrumental in acting as the launch pad of a large family-owned manufacturing empire. In 1885 the brothers Eugène and Armand, the third generation of the Peugeot family, transformed the company's fortunes, which up to then had produced only bicycles and tricycles, by starting car manufacture. Armand Peugeot had the foresight to predict that steam-driven cars had no future and turned his efforts to the design and production of petrol engines.

Peugeot's first motorcycles came in 1899. These were class-leading single and twin cylinder models, whose engines were so highly respected that they were also used by rival manufacturers. For example, the Norton with which Rem Fowler rode to victory in the first Tourist Trophy in 1907 had a Peugeot V-twin engine.

A new era at Peugeot began with the arrival of the Swiss engineer Ernest Henry who, after building successful Grand Prix cars, joined Peugeot in 1913 to design a new

parallel twin racer with a capacity of 498cc. A novelty was the valve gear, which not only used double overhead camshafts but 4 valves per cylinder. An entry by the factory in the 1913 French Grand Prix was planned to introduce the new bike, but instead Peugeot fielded the older V-twin.

With the outbreak of WWI all thoughts of racing were set aside for more serious pursuits. At the beginning of the 1920s the Romanian engineer Lessman Antionescu was hired to redesign the 1913 twin with the hindsight of new technology. The result was a simplified engine with only one camshaft and the number of valves reduced by half, while the geartrain now featured bevel gears and vertical shaft.

Although these measures appeared a backwards step, they succeeded, resulting in victory for Peugeot in the 1923 Grand Prix des Nations at Monza at an average speed of 75mph. On the roadster front Peugeot concentrated on side valve and overhead singles, plus later 2-strokes. After the rival firm of Terrot was taken-over in the 1950s production concentrated on 50cc machines, a policy continued today which sees Peugeot leading the way with a range of trend-setting scooters.

1902 Peugeot, 246cc, inlet over exhaust single cylinder, pedals, chain drive.
£3,500–4,000 *PC*

Peugeot continue to make two-wheelers (pedal cycles and powered mopeds, scooters and ultra-lightweight motorcycles) even to this day.

r. **1920s Peugeot Racer,** 350cc, overhead camshaft, twin port, chain final drive.
£20,000–22,000 *PC*

Leading Peugeot racing star of the early 1920s, Paul Pean on one of the factory's famous Grand Prix racers of the era. Today these are highly prized.

RALEIGH *(British 1899–1970s)*

1923 Raleigh 2¾hp, 399cc, single cylinder
side valve engine, chain-cum-belt final drive,
Sturmey-Archer gearbox with hand change
lever, girder forks, flat tank, luggage grid.
£2,000–2,200 *BKS*

r. **1926 Raleigh,** 349cc,
overhead valve single cylinder.
£2,200–2,400 *RSS*

1926 Raleigh Model 12, 798cc, side valve V-twin,
chain final drive, hand change, 3-speed gearbox.
£2,500–2,700 *RSS*

l. **1926 Raleigh,** 248cc, side valve single cylinder.
£2,300–2,500 *BKS*

*Although the Raleigh Cycle Co Ltd of Nottingham
offered an 800cc V-twin in their 1926 range, it was for
their lightweight 250cc and 350cc machines that the
company is best remembered. The side valve 248cc
bike of 1926 lived up to their contemporary advertising
slogan, 'Takes Everything in its Stride', and their
reliability is still proven in today's vintage events.*

RENE GILLET
(French 1898–1957)

1949 René Gillet MkVI, 124cc, 2-stroke single cylinder, 4 speed-gearbox, restored.
£450–650 *BKS*

Founded in 1898, the French firm of René Gillet built their reputation on large capacity singles, many of which were used by the French armed forces, characterised by extreme strength and stamina, but which had no sporting pretentions. Post-war production concentrated on lightweight 2-strokes such as the example shown here.

REX *(British 1900–33)*

1904 Rex, 346cc, stored, requires mechanical and safety checks.
£8,500–9,000 *BKS*

Rex began production in Birmingham in 1899 as motorcar and forecar manufacturers. A move to Coventry in 1900 saw the factory breaking new ground by exhibiting and proving a motorcycle at the Crystal Palace Show when their machine was the only one capable of climbing a nearby hill without pedal assistance. Following this formula and aided by a thorough advertising campaign the company continued to actively promote their products by, on one occasion, completing a record breaking Land's End to John O'Groats run in 1904.

RICKMAN *(British 1959–)*

l. **1971 Rickman Zündapp Lightweight,** 124cc, piston port 2-stroke single, air cooled.
£800–1,000 *BLM*

During the early 1970s the Rickman brothers, Don and Derek built and sold relatively large numbers of the 124cc Zündapp-engined motocross and enduro bikes, mainly in the USA, they also supplied a road version which was supplied to certain British police forces.

ROBINSON & PRICE *(British 1902–06)*

1903 Robinson & Price, 350cc, inlet over exhaust engine, belt final drive, vertical cylinder, pedal starting.
£8,500–9,000 *VER*

ROVER *(British 1902–25)*

1912 Rover 5hp Single Speed, side valve, single cylinder, belt final drive.
£6,000–7,000 *VER*

Although more famous for their cars, nonetheless the Rover company was one of the early pioneers of British motorcycling, building motorcycles from 1902 until 1925

ROYAL ENFIELD *(British 1901–70)*

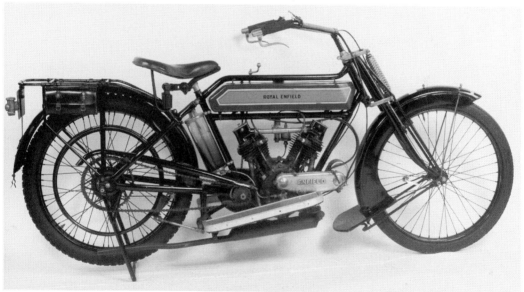

1915 Royal Enfield V-Twin, 425cc, overhead valve, variable speed, footboards, chain final drive, kickstart, glass oil tank.
£5,000–6,000 *BLM*

l. **1921 Royal Enfield 2¼hp,** restored, good condition.
£2,100–2,200 *BKS*

Like many other British motorcycle manufacturers, Royal Enfield's origins were in the bicycle trade. The Redditch company built its first powered vehicles – De Dion-engined tricycles and quadricycles – in the closing years of the 19thC, and its first motorcycle around 1900. By 1904 the firm was concentrating on car production, resuming motorcycle manufacture in 1910 with a V-twin Motosacoche-powered lightweight. A 2¼hp version with 2-speed gear followed. The marque's famous 6hp motorcycle combination was introduced in 1912 and the 3hp solo V-twin the year after. Enfield's first 2-stroke – the 2¼hp with 225cc single-cylinder engine and 2-speed gear – appeared in 1914. The model resumed production at the war's end and continued into the mid-1920s.

1946 Royal Enfield Model CO, 346cc,
overhead valve single cylinder, 70 x 90mm
bore and stroke, foot change, 4-speed gearbox,
girder forks, rigid frame.
£1,400–1,500 *BKS*

r. **1952 Royal Enfield RE2 'Flying Flea',** 126cc.
£500–600 *BKS*

*Derived from the pre-war RE model, that had been
produced at the request of the former Dutch DKW
importer, the RE2 introduced a number of changes
including telescopic front forks and a redesigned
engine of much cleaner appearance.*

1952 Royal Enfield Bullet, 350cc, overhead valve.
£1,500–1,800 *BLM*

*Enfield revived the Bullet name in 1948 for a sensational new 350
sports bike with swinging arm rear suspension. After their Colmore
Cup trials debut, the prototypes performed well at the ISDT later in
the year, and the production models duly arrived in 1949. The
newcomer featured an overhead-valve engine which housed its dry-
sump oil tank in a compartment in the rear of the crankcase, to
which the 4-speed gearbox was rigidly bolted in a form of semi-unit
construction. The Bullet came in road, trials, or scrambles versions,
with equipment and gearing to suit the application – there was
even a racer in the mid-1950s. A 500cc Bullet joined the range in
1953. Production of both Bullets ceased in 1962, the name passing
to the 350cc version of the unit-construction Crusader 250.*

1955 Royal Enfield Bullet, 346cc,
overhead valve single, 4-speed gearbox.
£1,800–2,000 *BKS*

1959 Royal Enfield Meteor Minor, 496cc, overhead valve vertical twin, 4-speed, short stroke, 70 x 64.5mm, 8:1 compression ratio, alternator, new clutch mechanism, Siamesed pipes, 17in wheels, requiring restoration.
£750–850 *AT*

The Meteor Minor ran from 1958 through to 1963.

1958 Royal Enfield Bullet, 500cc.
£1,700–2,000 *BKS*

The Bullet could be purchased in road, trials or scambles versions with equipment and gearing to suit. The 500cc Bullet was first produced in 1953 and production ceased in 1962, the name passing to the 350cc version of the unit construction Crusader 250.

> **Miller's is a price GUIDE not a price LIST**

1961 Royal Enfield Crusader Sports, 247cc, overhead valve unit construction single cylinder, 4-speed, chrome guards and alloy wheel rims.
£900–1,100 *PC*

r. **1962 Royal Enfield Crusader Sports,** 247cc, overhead valve single cylinder, chrome tank and mudguards, 4-speed, good condition.
£1,200–1,500 *M*

RUDGE (British 1911–40)

1913 Rudge Multi, 499cc, good condition.
£6,500–7,000 *VER*

Although famous for bicycles, Don Rudge did not begin motorcycle production until the launch of the single cylinder 500cc inlet over exhaust engined model in 1911. After success at Brooklands and the TT, Rudge produced the Multi (for multi-gear not cylinders) which was built both before and after WWI.

1936 Rudge Ulster Grand Prix, 499cc overhead valve twin port single comprehensive restoration.
£8,000–8,500 *BKS*

Introduced to celebrate Graham Walker's victory in the 1928 Ulster Grand Prix (at an average speed of over 80mph), Rudge's new Ulster model offered 90mph performance, comparable to the 'cammy' Norton and Velocette singles but without their fussiness, an excellent linked braking system, and fine handling.

1936 Rudge Special, 499c, overhead valve single, twin port foot change gearbox, good condition.
£2,300–2,500 *BKS*

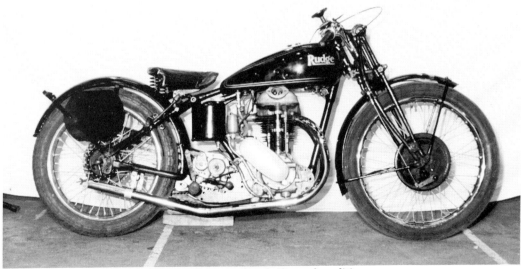

1938 Rudge Special Sport, 499cc, engine recently rebuilt, good condition.
£1,800–2,000 *PS*

This machine was used for many years with some success as a sprint machine.

SCOTT *(British 1909–69)*

Today the lightweight, water-cooled, 2-stroke, twin cylinder is the accepted formula for success in the 250cc Grand Prix racing category. Yet when Yorkshireman Alfred Angus Scott pioneered this design at the turn of the century it was branded an elaborate freak.

Alfred Scott had begun by developing a small 130cc 2-stroke engine as an auxiliary power unit for bicycles in 1902, but it was not until 1908 that he made a prototype of his twin cylinder 2-stroke. This original prototype, and, the early production models that came the following year, featured air-cooled cylinders and water-cooled heads. But soon water-cooling was used for both cylinders and heads.

The unusual cooling principle was not the only original feature of Scott's models. The engine featured a novel crankshaft, with both cranks having overhead connecting rods with the flywheel located between the cylinders. The 2-speed gearbox and the rear wheel both had chain drive. The fully triangulated frame was fitted with a new type of girder front fork, with a central spring, which was the forerunner of later telescopic forks.

Just how far in advance of the time these machines were is shown by the fact that three years in succession (1912–14) a Scott machine set the fastest lap in the Senior TT. The roadster and racing models were distinguished by the colour of their cylinders – red and green respectively.

The avant-garde nature of Scott's 2-strokes did not change after the death of its founder in 1923. Instead W. Cull continued technical development which now included 498 and 596cc models named the Squirrel, the larger model having a top speed of 85mph in roadster trim. Also worthy of mention are an air-cooled 297cc single cylinder (1929) and a large bore water-cooled 2-stroke 996cc model which appeared in 1934 and boasted a longitudinally arranged 3 cylinder in-line engine with an output of 50bhp.

In 1950 the company ceased production at its Shipley factory and, under the guidance of Matt Holder, moved to Birmingham where only very limited production was undertaken.

1929 Scott Squirrel, 300cc, air-cooled, sloping single cylinder.
£2,250–2,500 *BLM*

> **Don't Forget!**
> *If in doubt please refer to the 'How to Use' section at the beginning of this book.*

1928 Scott Flying Squirrel, 596cc, replacement cylinder block, detachable alloy head, good condition.
£3,900–4,200 *BKS*

Bradford-born Alfred Angus Scott's experiments with 2-stroke motorcycle engines began in the late 19th century. The first complete Scott motorcycle followed in 1908, its twin-cylinder engine, 2-speed footchange gear, and all chain drive marking it out as an advanced design for its day. Lightweight, ample power, and sure-footed handling thanks to a low centre of gravity, were Scott virtues right from the outset.

1929 Scott Flying Squirrel, 498cc, 2-stroke, twin cylinder, water-cooled, girder forks, coil spring suspension, rigid rear frame, sound condition.
£2,700–3,000 *BKS*

1929 Scott TT Replica, 498cc, 2-stroke, water-cooled, complete with pillion pad and headlamp. **£3,000–3,300** *BKS*

This particular example was first registered in Barnsley, South Yorkshire, in June 1929.

l. **1929 Scott Flying Squirrel**, 498cc, 3-speed gearbox, girder forks. **£2,500–3,000** *S*

This machine has been fitted with a period set of 'bolt-on' goodies including a pair of neatly engineered friction dampers.

r. **1930 Scott Super Squirrel**, 596cc, 2-stroke, twin cylinder, water-cooled, girder forks, fully complete and running example. **£2,800–3,200** *S*

Locate the Source

The source of each illustration in Miller's can be found by checking the code letters below each caption with the Key to Illustrations.

1929 Scott Flying Squirrel, 498cc, water-cooled twin engine, petrol drip tap to bleed carburettor, Andre steering damper, fitted clip for route map. **£3,200–3,500** *BKS*

The water-cooled twin engine provides a distinctive 'Scott yowl' unlike any other motorcycle.

1948 Scott Flying Squirrel, 596cc, stainless steel mudguards, original Burgess silencer and exhaust system. **£3,600–4,000** *BKS*

This example of the Shipley factory's early post-war production features Dowty Oleomatic forks that Scott specified as replacements for the girder forks initially supplied.
This machine was purchased in London 20 years ago and has reputedly completed less than 100 miles since.

1957 Scott Squirrel, 596cc, 2-stroke, water-cooled, 4-speed, foot change. **£4,000–4,500** *TDC*

Limited production of Scotts continued in the 1950s. This pristine example features telescopic forks, swinging arm rear suspension, full-width alloy brake hubs, dual seat and Siamesed exhaust system.

SUNBEAM *(British 1912–57)*

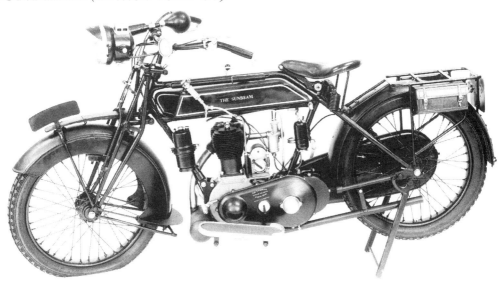

1920 Sunbeam 3½hp, side valve single cylinder, hand gearchange, excellent original condition, old duplicate log book, parts list and operating manual.
£3,800–4,200   *ELA*

1921 Sunbeam 3½hp, 500cc, overhead valve single cylinder.
£15,000–18,000   *MSR*

Machines like this won the Bol d'Or TT and Grand Prix des Nations during the early 1920s.

1923 Sunbeam Longstroke TT Sportsman, 492cc, Sunbeam oil-bath chaincase, rear carrier, older restoration, good condition.
£4,600–5,000   *BKS*

John Marston Ltd of Sunbeamland, Wolverhampton, marketed the 3.5hp Longstroke Sunbeam as 'The Speedman's Machine', the 77 x 105.5mm engine having high compression and special sports cams. The bike was equipped with sports handlebars and hand change 3-speed countershaft gearbox.

1924 Sunbeam 2¾hp, 350cc.
£6,000–7,000   *MSR*

Re-introduced for 1923, the 2¾hp model (350cc) was a capacity neglected by Sunbeam since 1914. A fairly mundane machine, its significance is that its design acted as the basis for other models of the same capacity, many with overhead valves for both road and racing use in the following decade.

1925 Sunbeam 3½hp, 492cc short-stroke side valve engine.
£5,500–6,000 *BKS*

Sunbeam's second model was the John Greenwood-designed 3½hp of 1913. A side valve single like its predecessor, the 3½hp came with a 3-speed handchange gearbox and fully enclosed oil bath chaincases, the latter first seen on the company's bicycles. Although effectively superseded by the famous long-stroke which appeared in 1921, the short-stroke (85 x 88mm) model remained in production until 1926. This example is believed to have been supplied by the factory to special order, and is almost certainly one of the last of Sunbeam's sports side valves to employ the short-stroke engine.

1925 Sunbeam Model 6, 492cc.
£4,800–5,200 *BKS*

Sunbeam's famous long-stroke (77 x 105.5mm) side valve engine first appeared at the 1921 French Grand Prix, scoring a debut win in the hands of Alex Bennett. In road-going form this remarkable engine remained in production right up until WWII. The Model 6 long-stroke had gained drum brakes by the mid-1920s, and in lightweight guise with low handlebars and minimal equipment, was known as the 'speedman's machine'.

1927 Sunbeam Model 9, 492cc, overhead valve single cylinder.
£4,200–4,600 *BKS*

The Model 9, an overhead valve 500cc touring machine, was but one of the machines which established the Sunbeam reputation and this flat tank example, first registered in Devon, is a good original example.

1927 Sunbeam Model 90, 493cc, overhead valve twin port single cylinder.
£10,300–11,500 *BKS*

This example of Sunbeam's overhead valve 500 racer dates from 1927, the year Sunbeam riders Graham Walker, Charlie Dodson and Dick Birch came away with the Manufacturer's Team Prize from the Isle of Man Senior TT.

1927 Sunbeam Model 9, 492cc, running order, unrestored.
£3,500–4,200 *RRN*

1927 Sunbeam Model 6, 492cc, side valve long-stroke tourer in light sports form, flat tanker, drum brakes, fully enclosed oil bath chaincase.
£3,600–4,000 *BKS*

1928 Sunbeam Model 90, 492cc twin port engine, crankcase supported by 3 ball bearings, dry-sump lubrication, primary drive enclosed in cast alloy chaincase, 3 speed 'cross-over-drive' gearbox, offside power take-off.
£8,600–9,400 *BKS*

Sunbeam had begun experimenting with overhead valves on their factory racers in the early 1920s, and these duly appear on production models in 1924. The new 500 roadster was known as the Model 9 while its race bike counterpart, which could top 90mph, was accordingly designated the Model 90.

l. **1928 Sunbeam Model 90,** 492cc, overhead twin port single cylinder.
£9,000–10,000 *MSR*

Don't Forget!

If in doubt please refer to the 'How to Use' section at the beginning of this book.

r. **1930 Sunbeam Model 90,** 492cc overhead valve racing engine, 3-speed footchange gearbox, saddle tank, modified front brake and clutch.
£5,300–5,800 *BKS*

This bike is one of the last 1930 Sunbeam 90s built, and features the low frame introduced in 1929.

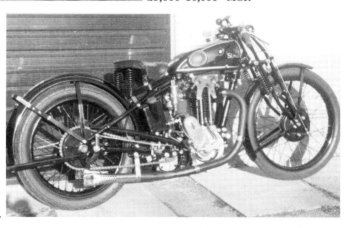

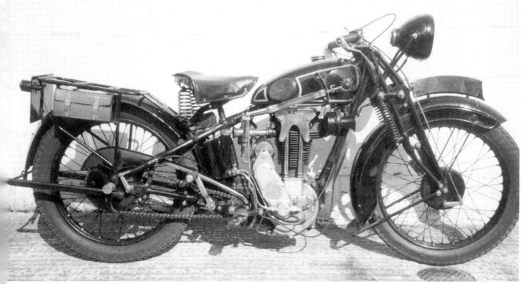

1930 Sunbeam Model 8, 348cc, overhead valve, 4-speed, hand change gearbox.
£2,750–3,000 *AT*

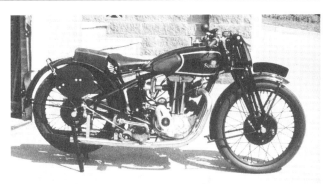

1930 Sunbeam Model 9,
492cc, overhead valve twin port
single cylinder.
£3,000–3,500 *BKS*

*During the late 1920s Sunbeam
followed the then fashionable trend to
twin port heads before reverting to a
single port design in 1934. Pushrod
enclosure had arrived in 1930, to be
followed a couple of years later by
partial enclosure of the rocker gear.*

1932 Sunbeam Model 90, 492cc, 8in diameter brakes, Amal
TT carburettor, modified gearbox, Norton footchange mechanism.
£3,900–4,200 *BKS*

*Sunbeam-manufactured Webbs forks differentiated the
Wolverhampton factory's 1931 onwards models from their
Druid-equipped predecessors. This Model 90 is believed to have
been raced at some time.*

1948 Sunbeam S7, 489cc, overhead camshaft, rubber mounted shaft drive in-line twin, coil ignition.
£2,500–3,000 *BLM*

r. **1950 Sunbeam
S7,** 489cc, overhead
camshaft in-line twin
with shaft final drive,
excellent condition.
£2,400–2,800 *BMM*

l. **1950 Sunbeam S8,** 489cc, requires restoration.
£950–1,100 *S*

*Following WWII, Sunbeams had been taken over by BSA.
They offered 2 models, the S7 and the S8. Both motorcycles
featured a 489cc vertical twin mounted in-line in a cradle
frame, with shaft drive to the rear wheel. The S7 endeavoured
to capture the quality of pre-war Sunbeams with its deeply
valanced mudguards and, with a possible eye on sales to
North America, they fitted balloon tyres. The S8 was a far
more spartan model; it was easy to spot a number of
components such as forks and hubs that it shared with the
more mundane BSA twins of the period.*

1951 Sunbeam S7, 489cc.
£2,300–2,500 *BKS*

1950 Sunbeam S7 De Luxe, 489cc, extra capacity sump, additional passenger seat, very good condition.
£3,400–3,800 *BKS*

The Sunbeam S7 was much admired for its innovative rear wheel shaft drive. Combined with a stylish valanced panelling usually finished in a light green, it was the ideal weather conscious touring machine of the 1950s which even to this day appeals to a wide following of enthusiasts. The S7 is distinctive by its use of unusually bulbous tyres, two-into-one exhaust and fluted silencer.

A wartime design by Erling Poppe, the Sunbeam in-line twin was launched by BSA – owners of Sunbeam Cycles Ltd – in 1946. Intended as a luxury tourer, it was of advanced specification with a rubber-mounted overhead camshaft engine, shaft drive, and plunger rear suspension. The first S7 version was equipped with 4.00 x 16 balloon tyres, a feature not incorporated into the deliberately more conventional – and also lighter and cheaper – S8 introduced in 1949. The S7 continued as the S7 de luxe, both models remaining in production until 1956.

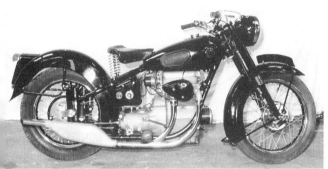

> **Did you know?**
> **MILLER'S Classic Motorcycles Price Guide** *builds up year-by-year to form the most comprehensive photo library system available.*

c1952 Sunbeam S8, 489cc.
£2,400–2,600 *BKS*

The S8 was a slightly leaner, more sporting variant of Sunbeam's post-war overhead camshaft, in-line, shaft drive twin.

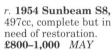

r. **1954 Sunbeam S8,**
497cc, complete but in
need of restoration.
£800–1,000 *MAY*

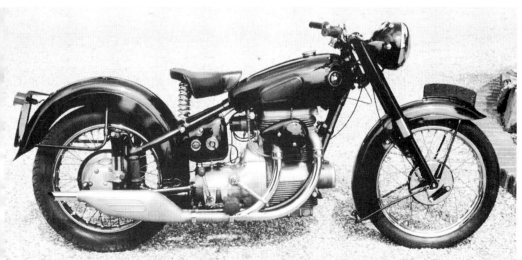

1957 Sunbeam S8, 489cc, overhead camshaft in-line twin, good condition.
£2,000–2,300 *VER*

SUZUKI *(Japanese 1952–)*

1968 Suzuki U50, 49.9cc, disc valve 2-stroke single, 3-speed, 17in wheels, 4.1bhp at 6000rpm.
£55–75 *BKS*

The U50 commuter machine – known largely as a 'step-thru' – of 1966–68 replaced the earlier M30 model. It was superceded by the F50 from 1969.

1973 Suzuki GT380, 371cc, 3 cylinder air-cooled 2-stroke, original drum brake model, non-standard front mudguard, running order, spare engine unit.
£800–1,000 *BKS*

Probably one of the best known of the 1970s sports machines from Japan, the GT380 used a 371cc 3 cylinder engine which possessed fierce acceleration for its capacity. Combined positive road handling and firm braking made this a popular machine for the sporting rider of the day.

1975 Suzuki RE5M, 497cc, single rotor oil and water-cooled Wankel engine, concours condition.
£3,000–3,300 *ROW*

The first RE5 version (RE5M) featured 'Rotary Theme' styling to the indicators, speedo and rear light. Later version (RE5A) had conventional items. Suzuki was the only Japanese company to place its Wankel project into full production. Some 5,000 RE5s were built between 1974 and 1977.

1977 Suzuki GS750, 748cc, double overhead camshaft, 5 speed, disc brakes front and rear.
£1,600–1,800 *MAY*

TERROT
(French 1901–early 1960s)

1927 Terrot 2¾hp, 349cc, overhead camshaft single, handchange, chain final drive, girder forks, rigid frame.
£3,400–3,800 *BKS*

1921 Raleigh Model 2¾hp, 399cc, good condition, fully restored, 3 owners since 1983.
£2,200–2,500 *BKS*

Raleigh machines dating from the vintage period are regarded as being soundly engineered and worthy.

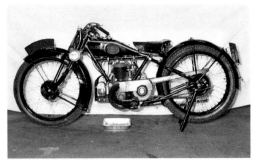

1929 Raleigh Model 15 De Luxe, 248cc.
£1,800–2,200 *PS*

1911 Rex 3½hp, side valve, single cylinder, 2-speed hub, fully restored.
£5,000–5,500 *AT*

1904 Rex, 346cc, single cylinder, belt final drive.
£9,000–10,000 *VER*

1922 Royal Enfield, 223cc, single cylinder, belt final drive, rear wheel braking.
£1,500–1,750 *PM*

1949 Royal Enfield RE, 126cc, 2-stroke single cylinder engine, 3.5bhp at 4500rpm.
£450–500 *BMM*

Civilian version of the wartime Flying Flea model, itself inspired by the pre-war German DKW RT125 design.

1950 Royal Enfield J2 Twin Port Single, 499cc.
£1,600–2,000 *BKS*

Royal Enfield first produced the J2 twin port overhead valve 499cc model for the home market in 1950. A certain amount of success had been enjoyed by Bill Lomas on home tuned Royal Enfield machines in the short circuit racing during 1949. It is believed this assisted home sales and prompted the introduction of the J2 into the market.

1951 Royal Enfield Bullet, 346cc, overhead valve single cylinder.
£1,600–1,800 *BLM*

The prototype Bullet appeared in the spring of 1948 at the Colmore Trial and later that year won gold medals as part of the successful British Trophy team in the ISDT.

1958 Royal Enfield Bullet, 499cc,
overhead valve single.
£2,500–2,800 *BLM*

*Known as the Big Head Bullet, due to the much
larger cylinder head than that used on the more
numerous 350cc version.*

1961 Royal Enfield Bullet, 346cc, single
cylinder, overhead valve, chrome tank and
mud guards, full width brakes hubs.
£1,500–2,000 *CONQ*

1965 Royal Enfield 250 GT, 247cc, overhead
valve single, 5-speed, clip-ons, swept tank
exhaust pipe, flyscreen.
£1,300–1,500 *PM*

*The GT was the epitome of the mid-1960s café
racer and a successful attempt by Enfield to
produce a machine which '60s youth wanted to
buy. Company chief Leo Davenport had taken
the trouble to ask his dealers what they wanted,
then built a prototype with the help of
enthusiastic apprentices at the Redditch factory.*

1938 Rudge Special, 499cc, 4-valve head,
enclosed valve gear, valenced muguards,
to original specification.
£3,700–4,000 *VER*

1960 Royal Enfield Constellation, 692cc,
overhead vertical twin, 70 x 90mm bore and stroke.
£2,500–3,000 *PS*

*In April 1958 Enfield announced two higher
performance versions of its 700 Meteor, the Meteor
Minor, and even the more highly tuned Constellation.
The 'Connie' as it was soon to be known produced
51bhp and was good for around 110mph.*

1964 Royal Enfield Crusader Sports, 247cc,
overhead valve, 4-speed.
£800–1,000 *BLM*

This has the correct painted tank, rather than chromed

1937 Rudge Special, 499cc, overhead valve single
cylinder with 4 parallel valves.
£3,300–3,600 *PS*

1938 Rudge Ulster, 499cc, single semi-radial
bronze head, twin port, overhead camshaft.
£4,500–5,000 *CONQ*

*The semi-radial 4-valve bronze cylinder
head became synonymous with this famous
model which took its name from the
company's racing successes in the
Ulster Grand Prix.*

1927 Scott Flyer, 498cc, 2-stroke, twin cylinder, water-cooled, good condition.
£5,250–5,850 *VER*

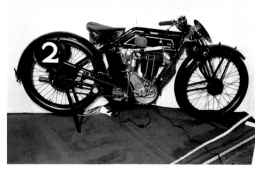

1926 Sunbeam Sprint, 492cc.
£14,000–15,500 *MSR*

1931 Sunbeam Model 5, 500cc, oil-bath chain guard.
£2,600–2,800 *BLM*

1932 Sunbeam Model 9, 492cc, replica 90 Special, overhead valve, twin port single.
£4,000–4,500 *MSR*

1952 Sunbeam S8, 497cc, restored, finished in gun-metal grey.
£2,250–2,500 *MAY*

1972 Suzuki TS90R, 89.9cc, disc valve 2-stroke, 5 gears, 11bhp at 7500rpm.
£575–650 *PS*

1972 Suzuki GT750, 736cc, 3-cylinder, water-cooled, 2-stroke, 70 x 64mm bore & stroke, 67bhp at 6500rpm.
£1,200–1,400 *BKS*
This is an example of the original drum brake model, in its first production year.

1973 Suzuki TT500, 493cc, piston port, 2-stroke, twin cylinder, air-cooled, 5-speed, 70 x 64mm, 46bhp at 7000rpm.
£1,200–1,500 *NLM*

TT500 was the sports version of Suzuki's big air-cooled twin. Although the standard T500/GT500 are still relatively plentiful, the TT variant is now very rare.

1926 Triumph Model P, 494cc, single valve, single cylinder.
£3,000–3,500 *BLM*

1928 Triumph TT Model, 498cc, overhead valve single cylinder, twin port, hi-level exhaust, Brooklands cans, ex-works, concours condition.
£7,800–8,500 *VER*

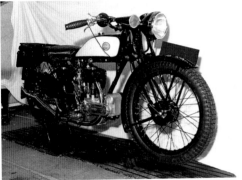

1930 Triumph NSD3, 550cc, side valve, single cylinder, restored, original wheel rims made by Palmer.
£2,500–3,000 *RRN*

1939 Triumph Tiger 100, 498.76cc, overhead valve, vertical twin, iron head and barrel, 34bhp at 7000rpm.
£2,700–3,300 *BLM*

First built in 1938, the T100 was the sports version of the 5T speed twin.

1950 Triumph 5T Speed Twin, 498.76cc, overhead valve twin cylinder, optional sprung hub, concours condition.
£3,500–4,000 *VER*

1955 Triumph 6T Thunderbird, 649cc, overhead valve twin cylinder, swinging arm, SU carburettor.
£3,000–3,500 *BLM*

1959 Triumph Tiger 100, 499cc, overhead valve twin cylinder.
£2,900–3,100 *BLM*
The Tiger 100 for 1959 had a splayed cylinder head and 2 Amal Monobloc carburettors. The front brake was without ventilation.

1959 Triumph Twenty One 3TA, 349cc, overhead valve unit construction, twin cylinder, 'bathtub' rear enclosure.
£2,250–2,500 *BLM*

1960 Triumph T110, 649cc, overhead valve
pre-unit twin cylinder.
£3,000–3,400 *CONQ*

*For the 1960 model year all the 650 Triumphs
received a new swinging arm frame with single
top loop and saddle tubes joined by duplex
downtubes passing under the engine. The 6T
and T110 also received rear end enclosure, and
deeply valanced front mudguard.*

1961 Triumph Bonneville Replica, 649cc,
overhead valve pre-unit twin cylinder,
duplex frame.
£2,500–3,000 *BLM*

1966 Triumph Tiger 90, 349cc, restoration project.
£1,250–1,500 *PS*

1966 Triumph T20 Tiger Cub, 199cc, overhead
valve, alloy head, 4-speed, points on side, correct
rear enclosure, good condition.
£800–1,000 *VER*

1960 Triumph T20S, 199cc, overhead valve
single cylinder.
£1,100–1,300 *PS*

*An embryo street scrambler, the T20S was
aimed very much at the American market,
with its heavy duty forks, direct lighting and
Amal Monobloc carburettor.*

1962 Triumph 5TA Speed Twin, 490cc,
overhead valve twin cylinder, excellent condition,
all matching numbers, full documents.
£2,500–3,000 *AT*

1966 Triumph Tiger 90, 349cc, overhead valve,
original specification.
£2,200–2,700 *BLM*

The sporting version of the Triumph unit 350.

1967 Triumph T90 Tiger 90, 349cc, overhead
valve twin cylinder.
£1,700–2,000 *PS*

1968 Triumph TR25W Trophy, 247cc, overhead valve unit, single cylinder, 67 x 70mm, 10:1 compression, 24bhp at 8000rpm.
£1,500–1,700 *BLM*

The TR25W was essentially a badge engineered BSA. The majority were exported to the USA.

1970 Triumph TR6C, 649cc, overhead valve, twin cylinder, 9:1 compression ratio.
£3,800–4,200 *GLC*

The TR6C was a street scrambler similar to the 500 T100C, but based on the Tiger 650 model.

1970 Triumph TR6 Trophy, 649cc, overhead valve unit, twin cylinder, single carburettor.
£2,800–3,200 *BKS*

Belonging to the last generation of Triumph twins built before BSA-Triumph switched to the Umberslade Hall-designed oil-in-the-frame models. This example has been partially restored.

1971 Triumph ISDT Replica, 560cc, overhead valve unit twin cylinder, built by Eric Cheney, nickel-plated chassis, excellent condition.
£3,500–4,500 *CROW*

1973 Triumph T150V, 740cc, overhead valve, 3-cylinder, 5-speed gearbox, disc front brake.
£2,500–3,500 *CONQ*

1973 Triumph TR5T Trophy Trail, 490cc.
£3,000–3,500 *BLM*

Trophy trails and adventurers were dual purpose bikes for both road and dirt. ISDT medal winners ridden by the likes of Ken Heanes.

1975 Triumph T140 V Bonneville, 740cc, non-standard Norton 'pea-shooter' silencers, 67 x 70mm bore and stroke, 10in disc brake, 44bhp at 6500rpm.
£2,500–3,250 *CROW*

1977 Triumph T140V Bonneville, 740cc, US specification, Hagon shocks, alloy chainguard, Norton silencers, otherwise original specification.
£2,500–3,500 *CONQ*

1925 Velocette Model G, 249cc, 2-stroke, single cylinder, 3-speed gearbox, footboards, rear carrier.
£1,800–2,000 *VER*

1936 Velocette KSS MkII, 348cc, overhead camshaft.
£3,500–4,500 *CROW*

First introduced in 1925, the KSS was the super sports variant of Velocette's first post-WWI 4-stroke, the overhead camshaft Model K.

1949 Velocette MkI LE, 149cc, water-cooled, side valve, twin cylinder.
£600–700 *LEV*

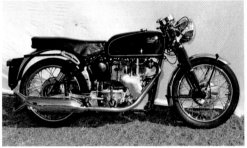

1954 Velocette MAC, 349cc, overhead valve single cylinder, concours condition.
£3,000–3,200 *Velo*

This machine has been converted to Viper specification. It has a later 2LS front brake from Thruxton model.

1954 Velocette MAC, 349cc.
£1,800–2,500 *Velo*

In touring trim with screen and panniers. The MAC (and 500 MSS) were the workhorses of the Velocette 4-stroke range.

1958 Velocette Venom, 499cc, overhead valve single cylinder, chrome guard, fishtail silencer, fully restored.
£3,000–3,400 *ABT*

The British Racing Green paintwork is as the original specification from the Hall Green factory.

1960 Velocette Valiant, 192cc, air-cooled overhead valve, twin cylinder, horizontally opposed cylinders, shaft final drive, leading axle front forks.
£1,200–1,500 *LEV*

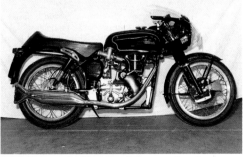

1960 Velocette Venom, 499cc, overhead valve single cylinder, Michenhall fairing, alloy rims, 2LS front brake.
£3,300–3,600 *TDC*

The engine is to Thruxton specification.

1950 Vincent Series C Comet, 499cc, overhead valve, single cylinder, fully restored.
£4,500–5,000 *AT*

Production of the Series C Comet got under way in the spring of 1949, after making its debut at the London Earl's Court Show the previous year.

1955 Vincent Series D Rapide, 998cc, 50° V-twin, overhead valve.
£13,000–15,000 *CONQ*

The original Series D V-twin was seen by Philip Vincent as the ultimate 'gentleman's motorcycle'. Unfortunately, its full enclosure was not to everyone's liking and after suffering problems with the fibreglass bodywork, some machines were completed 'naked'.

1922 Wolf 2½hp, 293cc, inlet over exhaust JAP single cylinder engine, 2-speed handchange.
£2,000–2,500 *AT*

1979 Yamaha RD 400E, 398cc, 2-stroke twin cylinder.
£900–1,100 *ARD*

This is the final version of the popular RD series. There was also an American market Daytona Special, coded RD 400F. This was the last Yamaha 2-stroke roadster to be imported into the USA.

1951 Vincent Series C Comet, 499cc.
£3,500–3,800 *BKS*

The Comet proved reliable in service and could cruise all day at 70mph, whilst giving 70mpg – excellent figures indeed. This machine, although not in concours condition, is 'ready to ride'.

1974 Yamaha RD 125, 124cc, 2-stroke twin cylinder, 43 x 43mm, 16bhp at 8500rpm, 5-speed, in process of being restored.
£300–350 *ARD*

Incomplete, requires exhaust and silencers, otherwise almost ready to go.

1977 Yamaha XS650, 653cc, double overhead camshaft twin cylinder, 5-speed.
£1,500–1,800 *BKS*

Largely built by Yamaha for the American market, the XS650 was seen as Japan's answer to the Triumph Bonneville.

1977 Yamaha RD 400, 398cc, air-cooled, 2-stroke twin cylinder, 64 x 62mm, 6-speed.
£650–800 *ARD*

The air-cooled RD 400 was highly rated during its lifetime. 40bhp at 7000rpm gave 100mph plus performance and rapid acceleration.

1921 Alcyon Autocycle, 98cc, 2-stroke, single cylinder, chain final drive, period oil headlamp.
£500–550 *NAC*

1950 Trojan Minimotor, 49cc.
£800–1,000 *NAC*

This is an almost unique tandem engined machine.

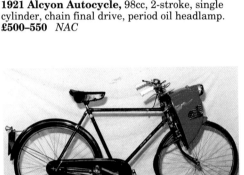

1952 Cymota Cycle Motor, 48cc.
£250–350 *NAC*

1957 New Hudson Autocycle, 49cc, hand-painted, requires restoration.
£100–150 *BMM*

c1954 AJS Replica Trials, 348cc, overhead valve single cylinder, alloy wheel rims.
£1,250–1,300 *BLM*

Built-up using a mixture of competition and roadster components.

1955 DOT TDHX Trials, 197cc, 2-stroke Villiers single cylinder engine, concours condition.
£1,250–1,500 *PC*

The Earles-type front fork became available on the production TD model midway through 1954, but only on models with swinging arm rear suspension. These forks were manufactured in Reynolds 531 tubing.

c1958 Ansel JAP Speedway, 349cc, JAP overhead valve engine, 3-stud cylinder head, alloy barrel, AMC gearbox.
£800–900 *BKS*

1958 Antig JAP Speedway, 499cc, overhead valve JAP engine with total loss oil supply, 3-speed Norton gearbox.
£950–1,200 *BKS*

1958 Greeves 24TA Scottish, 246cc, 31A Villiers engine, short 5¼in conrod, short barrel.
£1,000–1,200 *GRA*

This was the first year of the famous Scottish model, and was also available as the 20TA with 197cc motor.

1963 Greeves 24 TES Mk2, 246cc, 2-stroke single cylinder, Villiers 32A engine, complete but requires restoration.
£1,200–1,400 *BLM*

1966 BSA A50 Wasp, 499cc, overhead valve unit twin cylinders, hi-level open pipes, concours condition.
£4,200–4,400 *BOC*

American market model, high performance off-road machine.

1974 Bultaco Sherpa T350, 326cc, single cylinder, air-cooled, 2-stroke, 9:1 compression, 5-speed, 25mm Amal concentric carburettor, 21bhp at 5000rpm.
£350–400 *PS*

1960 BSA C15T Trials, 247cc, overhead valve unit construction, single cylinder, correct steel tank.
£1,000–1,250 *BLM*

1966 Cotton Trials, 247cc, Villiers 32A iron-barrelled engine, metal profiles, Ceriani-type telescopic forks, full width hubs, alloy guards, steel tank.
£1,000–1,200 *BLM*

1971-72 Villa Motocross, 125cc, 2-stroke air-cooled engine, 6-speed, original good condition.
£400–550 *PC*

These bikes were designed and built in Italy by the Villa brothers, Francesco and Walter.

1977 Honda TL125, 124cc, overhead camshaft unit construction, single cylinder.
£450–500 *PS*

Very original example of Honda's 'clubman' trials mount, including correct silencer and lighting equipment.

1941 BSA M20, 499cc, side valve single, magneto ignition, 7in brakes, 19in wheels, military specification with desert air filter and pannier bags.
£1,750–2,500 *CROW*

1940/45 BSA M20, 496cc, single valve, single cylinder, unused 1979 engine, magneto and gearbox.
£1,200–1,400 *BKS*

This is a genuine ex-War Department machine.

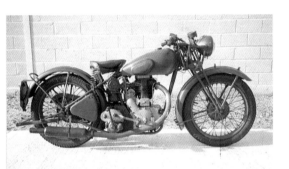

1945 Royal Enfield WD CO, 346cc, overhead valve single cylinder, 70 x 90mm, 4-speed footchange, magneto ignition.
£1,800–2,000 *BLM*

1939–45 Harley-Davidson WLA 45, 23bhp at 4500rpm, side valve V-twin, 3-speed, bottom link front suspension, rigid frame, restored.
£6,000–7,000 *RRM*

The WLA was an American-built machine.

1955 Heinkel Perle, 49cc, excellent condition.
£200–250 *BMM*

This German machine featured a unique alloy frame.

1957 Bown Moped, 47cc, German Sachs engine, trailing link front suspension.
£300–400 *NAC*

Very few examples of this model survive today.

1970 BSA Ariel, 49cc, Dutch Anker 2-stroke engine.
£110–130 *PS*

The Ariel 3 was one of the greatest of all BSA group failures.

1974 Puch Maxi Sport, 49cc, horizontal air-cooled 2-stroke.
£100–150 *MAY*

During the 1970s the Austrian Puch Maxi series was Europe's top selling moped.

1938 Norton Inter Racer, 490cc, overhead camshaft, footchange, 4-speed, girder forks, rigid frame.
£6,000–6,500 *BLM*

1953 Matchless G45, 498cc, overhead valve vertical twin, 66 x 72.8mm bore and stroke, original specification.
£14,000–16,000 *VER*

The G45 was derived from the Matchless G9 roadster twin cylinder, the '45' referring to its planned 45bhp.

1954 Matchless G45, 498cc, overhead valve twin cylinder, Burman racing gearbox, fully restored to original specification, concours condition.
£15,000–17,000 *GB*

The G45 was the work of H. J. (Ike) Hatch and was placed in production during early 1953.

1958 Norton 30M Manx, 499cc, double overhead camshaft, 86 x 85.62mm, 8in 2LS front brake, fully restored to concours condition.
£12,000–14,000 *NOC(C)*

1958 was the first year the Manx used the AMC gearbox. CRMC approved silencer, front brake airscoop.

1962/97 Matchless G50 Replica, 496cc, single overhead camshaft, 4 or 5-speed close ratio gearbox.
£21,200–23,500 *GB*

1959 Morini Setebello Style Racer, 174cc, overhead valve, tuned engine, 4-speed gearbox.
£800–1,000 *PS*

1966 Greeves RDS Silverstone, 246cc, piston port, 2-stroke, single cylinder, 66 x 72mm, 31bhp at 7500rpm, 5-speed Albion close ratio gearbox.
£2,800–3,000 *GRA*

1967 Bridgestone TAI, 191cc, twin cylinder disc valve, 2-stroke.
£1,200–1,400 *PS*

Race-kitted in the USA, including increasing the original capacity from 177cc. In 1992 it was comprehensively rebuilt by Sabre Racing for display in the UK on the Bridgestone stand at the 1992 NEC Motorcycle Show.

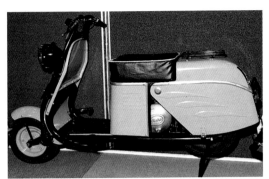

1949 Swallow Gadabout, 122cc, Villiers 9D
2-stroke engine, 3-speed.
£600–650 *VMSC*

*Swallow was a famous British sidecar builder which
ventured into the scooter market in the early 1950s.*

1955 Lambretta D150, 148cc, longer stroke
57 x 58mm.
£1,600–1,800 *VMSC*

1958 Lambretta LD150 MkIII, 147cc, single cylinder
2-stroke, shaft final drive, engine supported by pivoting
links and suspended at the rear by a single damper.
£850–950 *BKS*

1959 Lambretta Li Series 1, 148cc.
£1,000–1,300 *MAY*

*This is the first of the famous Li series,
built in both 125 and 150cc engine sizes.*

1961 Jawa Manet, 98cc, 2-stroke single cylinder.
£450–600 *JCZ*

1962 James Scooter, 149cc.
£500–600 *PM*

*The James company specialised in light-
weight motorcycles, and a scooter powered by
an AMC 149cc 2-stroke engine with horizontal
cylinder made its debut in 1960, allowing it to
be mounted directly under the floorboards.*

1964 Vespa Sportique 312L2, 125cc,
rotary valve engine.
£650–750 *MAY*
*British production of Vespas ended in 1963/64,
after which Douglas continued to import Piaggio
built models.*

1966 Lambretta Pacemaker 150, 148cc.
£750–850 *MAY*

*The Li special Pacemaker ran from 1963
through to 1966.*

1924 Rudge, 499cc, fitted with a Gloria sidecar, supplied by Charnwood.
£6,500–7,000   *CCR*

1927 Norton Model 19 with Norton Sidecar, 588cc.
£8,000–9,000   *PC*

1947 Norton 16H with Watsonian single seater sidecar, 490cc, single valve single cylinder, rebuilt.
£2,700–2,900   *NOC*

1959 Maico Maicoletta with Watsonian Bambini MkIII sidecar, 247cc, single cylinder 2-stroke.
£2,000–2,500   *MOC*

1956 BMW R60 with Steib Sports sidecar, 596cc.
£6,000–6,600   *CCR*

1957 Norton Inter/Manx Special, 490cc, single overhead camshaft engine.
£3,500–4,000   *NOC(C)*

1961 Greeves/Triumph Special, 490cc, Greeves roadster chassis with unit construction Triumph 5TA engine.
£1,500–2,000   *GRA*

This was originally built to take part in the Stella Alpine Rally.

1982 Motodd Laverda MkIV Special, 981cc, double overhead camshaft, 3 cylinder.
£4,000–5,000   *PC*

The original MkIV Motodd Laverda, as developed by Phil Todd, was raced with considerable success by Martin Routley. This road version uses the same 3 cylinder Jota-based engine with Saxon-made frame and suspension.

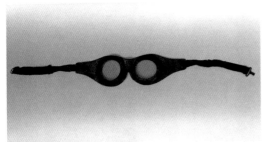

A pair of leather goggles, early 1920s, very good condition.
£25–30 *SW*

A Westwood rear lamp and a Motex motorcycle lamp, c1900.
£50–60 *LF*

A pair of leather gloves, original condition, 1930s.
£30–40 *SW*

A leather helmet, original condition, 1920s.
£40–50 *SW*

'Cocking a Snoop', a chrome motorcycle mascot, 1930s, 4in (10cm) high.
£50–65 *COB*

A metal kit model of a 1960 Triumph Pre-Unit Bonneville, manufactured 1970s, 9in (23cm) wide.
£350–400 *LE*

A steel advertising sign, featuring a BSA Gold Star, 1959, 16in (40.5cm) wide.
£10–12 *LF*

A steel advertising sign, featuring a Brough-Superior, 1930s, 15in (38cm) wide.
£10–12 *LF*

A signed photograph of Barry Sheen, 1978, 8 x 12in (20.5 x 30.5cm).
£50–75 *GPT*

Motor Cycling magazine,
Wednesday 15th October 1902,
11 x 8in (28 x 20.5cm).
£18–20 *DM*

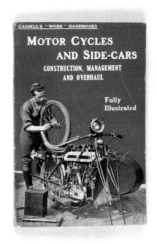

Motor Cycles and Side-Cars,
fully illustrated, published
by Cassell's, 1923,
7½ x 5in (19 x 13cm).
£15–18 *DM*

*Royal Enfield, The Joy of
the Road* brochure, 1931,
9 x 4½in (23 x 11.5cm).
£17–20 *DM*

*The 1931 Unapproachable
Norton* brochure, 9½ x 5½in
(24 x 14cm).
£25–30 *DM*

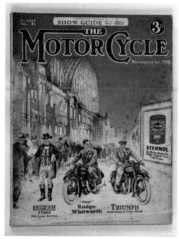

The Motor Cycle special
show guide, 1928,
11 x 8in (28 x 20.5cm).
£13–15 *DM*

*Good reference material
relating to older motorcycles
is becoming very collectable.*

Triumph single cylinder
maintenance and repair series,
covering 1937–61 models,
7½ x 5in (19 x 13cm).
£12–14 *DM*

Two copies of *The Motor Cycle* magazine,
1950s, 14 x 12in (35.5 x 30.5cm).
£3–6 each *COB*

The Excelsior Heinkel Tourist brochure,
1956, 10 x 8in (25.5 x 10cm).
£4–5 *DM*

TRIUMPH *(British 1902–)*
Launch of the 650 Thunderbird

In September 1949 Triumph launched their first 650 twin, the Thunderbird. This was a machine designed primarily for sustained high speeds on the vast, smooth highways of America, South Africa and Australia. With almost a third more power and a total weight of little more than that of the famous Speed Twin, the newcomer caused a big stir at the time.

Triumph picked the Montlhéry Autodrome, near Paris, to run a publicity coup with the first three machines off the Meriden factory's production line. Fully equipped, they were subjected to the most severe standard machine test held in the immediate post-war era. What was more, the test was a total success, the three bikes each covering 500 miles at an average speed of 92.23, 92.48 and 92.33mph respectively. The date of this demonstration of high speed reliability was the 29 September 1949, witnessed by Triumph chief Edward Turner, who was on hand to congratulate the team of five riders – Alex Scobie, Len Baylis, Syd Manns, Allan Jefferies and P. H. Alves. Under the supervision of the famous sidecar man and later British motocross team boss, Harold Taylor, the trio of Thunderbirds ran without problems throughout the test, which at the end of the 500 miles included a flying lap at over 100mph.

At the end of each machine's 500 miles there was very little externally to reveal the high speed work they had just completed.

The test had actually begun a couple of days before the Montlhéry performance, when the machines, fitted with panniers, set out from the works near Coventry. They were ridden through London en route to Folkestone and, on landing in France, they were ridden again to Montlhéry. The panniers were then removed, and for the purposes of the speed test Dunlop racing tyres were fitted (for safety reasons). Other changes amounted to revised saddles, rear set foot controls and the removal of the kickstart lever (so push starts were necessary), plus racing plugs, larger main jets, stronger clutch springs, and that was about it.

The Montlhéry track at that time was very bumpy and had a concrete surface. It measured 1.583 miles per lap and had steeply banked curves (like Brooklands) at either end. The track had such an immense width that the first time a machine was taken round it was difficult to know which way to point!

After this success, Triumph ran an advert which proclaimed '3 x 90 x 500! Thunderbird Introduces Itself!' It was something of which the British marque could be truly proud.

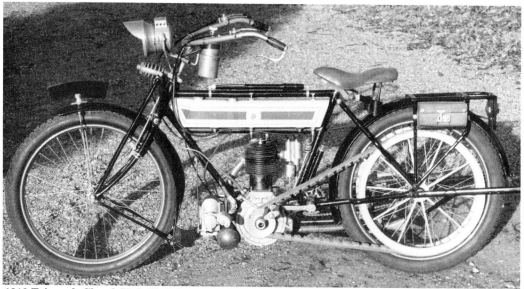

1913 Triumph Clutch/Hub Model,
500cc, inlet over exhaust single, vertical cylinder, belt final drive.
£5,500–6,000 *VER*

Don't Forget!
If in doubt please refer to the 'How to Use' section at the beginning of this book.

r. **1914 Triumph Model A,**
500cc, 3-speed, belt final drive.
£6,000–6,500 *VER*

1918 Triumph Junior, 225cc, 2-stroke.
£2,300–2,500 *BKS*

*Triumph produced their baby model
intending to appeal to those riders
requiring a lightweight conventional
machine. Introduced in 1913 and correctly
named the Junior it was a 225cc 2-stroke
with no pedal kick-start but incorporating
a 2-speed gear operated by a lever
mounted on the handlebars. The machine
was designed by Charles Hallaway.*

1919 Triumph Junior, 225cc, 2-stroke.
£1,800–2,000 *BMM*

The Junior is also known as the 'Baby'.

c1922 Triumph Ricardo, 4 valve, twin port overhead
valve port single, Harry Ricardo designed model.
£6,000–6,500 *AtMC*

1923 Triumph Model R, 3½hp,
4 valve single cylinder.
£4,200–4,600 *BKS*

*Triumph's early output was confined to side
valve machines, but in 1921 the Coventry
firm's first overhead valve model caused
a sensation. Based on the existing SD
('spring drive') model, the newcomer sported
a 4 valve cylinder head designed by Harry
Ricardo. Although the 'Riccy' was
unsuccessful at the Isle of Man TT races,
a works bike ridden by Frank Halford broke
the world flying mile record in 1921 with a
speed of 83.91mph. Although Rudge went on
to make a success of their 4 valve designs,
Triumphs did not last into the 1930s.*

c1925 Triumph Model P,
494cc, single valve single.
£2,750–2,950 *BKS*

*This machine is an example of Triumph's
famous Model P 494cc side valve single
that created a sensation when it was
introduced in 1925 at £42.12.6d, thereby
undercutting every other 500cc model on
the market. Despite its low price, the model
was equipped with a 3-speed, hand-
operated gearbox and all chain drive, as
well as a carrier and toolbox.*

1927 Triumph Model P, 494cc, side valve single, 3-speed, hand change, chain final drive.
£2,000–2,400 *AT*

1927 Triumph TT, 498cc, overhead valve single cylinder, complete, needing restoration.
£5,500–6,000 *PM*

1928 Triumph Model P, 493cc, single valve single cylinder, hand gearchange, rigid frame, girder forks.
£1,800–2,000 *S*

1938 Triumph Speed Twin, 498.76cc, overhead valve vertical twin, 63 x 80mm, 4-speed, 26bhp at 6000rpm, concours condition.
£6,000–6,500 *VER*

1938 Triumph Tiger 80, 343cc, overhead valve single, 70 x 89mm, 7.5:1 compression, 20bhp at 5700rpm.
£3,000–3,300 *BKS*

Built in 250, 350 and 500cc versions, the pre-war Tiger single series were individually tuned, tested, dismantled, inspected and reassembled before they were allowed to leave the factory.

1937 Triumph Tiger 80 Sport, 343cc, overhead valve single cylinder, 70 x 89mm, 20bhp at 5700rpm, excellent condition, restored.
£3,200–3,500 *PC*

1938 Triumph Tiger 80, 343cc, overhead valve single port, needing restoration.
£1,800–2,000 *PS*

1938 Triumph Tiger 70, 249cc, overhead valve single cylinder.
£2,100–2,300 *BKS*

Edward Turner's arrival at Triumph in 1936 resulted in extensive improvements to the range. A brilliant stylist, Turner transformed the Val Page-designed overhead valve singles by adopting sports specification engines, high level exhausts, chromed fuel tanks, and a new name – Tiger. Frames, forks, engines and gearboxes were all improved for 1937, and a trio of randomly selected Tigers successfully completed a series of arduous speed trials to secure the Maudes Trophy for Triumph later in the year.

1939 Triumph 3S, 349cc, side valve single cylinder, foot change, good condition.
£1,700–1,900 *BMM*

l. **1948 Triumph Tiger 100,** 498.76cc, overhead valve twin.
£2,900–3,100 *BKS*

This particular machine was originally exported to Malta in 1948.

1946 Triumph 5T Speed Twin, 498.76cc, overhead valve twin, 28bhp at 6000rpm, concours condition, fully restored, telescopic forks, rigid frame, 2 owners from new.
£2,900–3,200 *RRN*

1951 (registered 1952) Triumph Tiger 100, 499cc, overhead valve twin, alloy head and barrel, fully restored to factory original specification, 63 x 80mm bore and stroke, sprung hub, 7in front brake.
£3,500–4,000 *PC*

This machine was winner of Gorefield Show Concours in 1997.

1956 Triumph Tiger 100, 499cc, revised tank badge, 3 owners from new, matching engine and frame numbers.
£2,900–3,100 *BKS*

The sports version of Edward Turner's trend-setting Speed Twin 500, the Tiger 100 was launched in 1938. When production resumed in 1946, the T100 re-appeared with telescopic forks in place of the the original girders, and separate dynamo and magneto instead of the pre-war version's magdyno. An alloy cylinder head and barrel were adopted for 1951, these and other engine improvements boosting power to 32bhp. A swinging arm frame and 8in diameter front brake (first seen on the 649cc Tiger 110) were standard equipment from 1954 onwards.

1950 Triumph Thunderbird, 649cc.
£4,000–4,400 *BKS*

It was Edward Turner who named the 6T model the Thunderbird and it is said that he took this from native American mythology. Without doubt this was because Triumph always had an eye towards the American market. This undoubtedly assisted in establishing the Triumph legend in the USA and in fact it was the Americans themselves who adopted the name for one of their most famous sports cars.
The vertical twin engined Triumph was equipped with the famous Triumph sprung rear hub and the machine became as famous as any they produced. Perhaps it was the film The Wild One *in which Marlon Brando rode a Thunderbird that assisted the machine to attain its legendary status.*

1954 Triumph TR5 Trophy, 499cc.
£3,800–4,200 *BKS*

Triumph's TR5 Trophy model was introduced into the range in 1949 as a specialist trials machine developed from the company's own ISDT machines.

1957 Triumph 5T Speed Twin,
499cc, fully restored in 1978, stored
since 1988, fitted with Tiger 100
engine and 'slickshift' gearbox.
£2,300–2,500 *BKS*

c1957 Triumph Speed Twin, 499cc.
£2,600–2,900 *BLM*

*For 1957 the Speed Twin (and Thunderbird) retained the SU
carburettor, nacelle and iron head, but gained new petrol tank
styling, swinging fork frame and coil ignition.*

1958 Triumph 3TA Twenty One,
349cc, overhead valve unit construction
twin, 4-speed, totally restored, only
13 miles since restoration.
£2,700–3,000 *S*

Miller's is a price GUIDE
not a price LIST

1958 Triumph Thunderbird 6T, 649cc, overhead valve
twin, iron head and barrel, full width front hub, swinging
arm rear suspension.
£3,000–3,500 *BLM*

**1958 Triumph 6T
Thunderbird,** 649cc,
overhead valve twin,
iron head and barrel.
£2,800–3,100 *BLM*

r. **1959 Triumph T20
Tiger Cub,** 199cc,
overhead valve unit
construction single.
£600–800 *BLM*

*The 149cc Terrier was the
forerunner of the larger
capacity Cub, which
followed it into production
at the end of 1953. Early
models shared the
Terrier's plunger frame,
with the swinging arm
frame arriving in 1957.*

1961 Triumph Trophy, 649cc.
£2,500–2,700 *BKS*

This pre unit TR6 Trophy was similar to a Bonneville in general specification with a 8:1 compression ratio and a vertical twin engine which developed 40bhp at 6500rpm. Its main difference from the Bonneville at that time was the use of a single carburettor. During the 1960s the TR6 actually built up a formidable record of competition success in the USA which in effect continued its development from the early 1950s when the Trophy was developed for the International Six Day Trials.

r. **1963 Triumph Bonneville T120,** 649cc.
£2,900–3,100 *BKS*

Triumph entered the 1960s with its larger twin-cylinder machines recognisably similar to the first Speed Twin of 1938. Unit construction of engine and gearbox was already a feature of the 350 and 500 twins though, and the innovation duly appeared on the 650s in 1963.

1961 Triumph T100A, 490cc.
£2,200–2,400 *BKS*

Introduced for the 1960 season, the Tiger 100A was the sports version of Triumph's first unit-construction 500 twin, the 5TA. A raised compression ratio and 'hotter' cams helped the Tiger to a top speed in the region of 90mph, while the retention of a single carburettor meant that fuel economy did not suffer unduly, a gallon of fuel lasting for around 80 miles of restrained riding.

1962 Triumph Twenty One 3TA, 349cc, overhead valve twin, 4-speed gearbox, 'bathtub' rear enclosure, unrestored, but very clean.
£1,500–1,800 *PC*

Early in 1957 Triumph announced a new unit construction twin cylinder engined machine, which revived interest in the 350cc class. The newcomer was called the Twenty One – to celebrate the twenty first birthday of the Triumph Engineering Company and the useful fact that in the USA a 350cc engine was known as 21 cubic inches.

1962 Triumph 200 S/H Sports Cub, 199cc, overhead valve single cylinder, 9:1 compression, 63 x 64mm bore and stroke, 14.5bhp at 6500rpm.
£1,500–1,750 *AT*

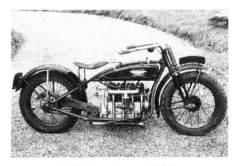

1967 Triumph T120R Bonneville, 649cc, fully restored to concours condition.
£4,000–4,400 *BLM*

This Bonneville was won with a £1 coin in a Classic Bike *magazine 'Spot the Ball' competition. The winner though didn't take the machine due to age, and no licence. An 'as new' example of one of motorcycling's great motorcycles.*

r. **1968 Triumph TR6R,** 649cc, high rise handlebars, original condition, 2LS front brake, non-original paintwork.
£2,000–2,600 *CROW*

1968 Triumph T100c, 490cc, overhead valve twin, 9:1 compression ratio, 38bhp at 7000rpm.
£2,800–3,300 *BLM*

Built for the USA, but later sold (albeit in small numbers) on the home market. Designed for enduro use with energy transfer ignition (UK models had 12 volt coil ignition).

1970 Triumph T150 Trident, oversize 1000cc engine, 3 cylinder, 5-speed, 4LS front brake, 'Raygun' silencers, alloy rims.
£4,500–5,000 *GLC*

Very similar to works machines used by TT marshalls.

1971 Triumph X75 Hurricane, 740cc, overhead valve, 3 cylinders.
£9,000–10,000 *TRI*

*The 'big tank' Euro-style had never appealed much to bike riders in the USA and as this was
BSA/Triumph groups largest market the company decided on a bold initiative – undertaken by the USA's
BSA West Coast office. This saw American designer Craig Vetter customise the BSA/Triumph 3-cylinder
model – as the revolutionary Hurricane with its 3 pipe exhaust and snappy bodywork. This is one of the few
surviving examples in showroom condition.*

1975 Triumph T160 Trident, 740cc,
US specification triple cylinder.
£3,000–3,500 *CONQ*

*In 1975 the T150 became the T160 with BSA
sloping style cylinders, duplex primary chain, left
side gear pedal, electric starter, 4-into-2 exhaust
and rear disc brake.*

1976 Triumph T160 Trident, 740cc, 5-speed,
58bhp at 7250rpm, electric start.
£3,000–3,500 *BLM*

1978 Triumph T140V, 740cc, overhead valve unit
twin, 5-speed gearbox.
£2,000–2,200 *CStC*

c1980 Triumph T140E, 744cc,
Vetter-type exhaust, good condition.
£3,000–3,500 *AtMC*

r. **1978 Triumph Bonneville 750,** 740cc, Meriden
Co-op built machine, original UK specification.
£2,200–2,400 *CStC*

VAN VEEN *(Dutch / German 1978–81)*

l. **1977 Van Veen OCR1000**, 996cc, twin rotor (2 x 498cc) oil and water-cooled Wankel engine.
£10,000+ *ROW*

The OCR1000 was the creation of the Dutch Kreidler importer (and race team), built in Germany, with an engine constructed by Comotor in Luxembourg. Maybe it should have been called the Euro Motorcycle Project! Only 49 were built in the late 1970s. Although some additional ones have been built since from spare parts. The price new, in 1977, was £7,500.

VELOCETTE *(British 1904–68)*

1922 Velocette Model E, 2-stroke, 3-speed gearbox, superb original condition, including duplicate log book, V5 registration form, parts list and instruction manual.
£4,500–5,000 *ELA*

1935 Velocette MAC, 349cc, overhead valve single.
£2,500–2,700 *BKS*

Renowned for engineering excellence in production of their single cylinder motorcycles, Velocette introduced the MAC as their medium capacity touring mount. It was fitted with a reliable 350cc single cylinder overhead valve engine and remained in their production line up right into the 1950s when it was superseded by the Viper.

1937 Velocette KSS, 348cc, overhead camshaft single cylinder.
£2,800–3,000 *S*

This machine has remained unused for many years, having been on display at the Totnes Motor Museum, Devon.

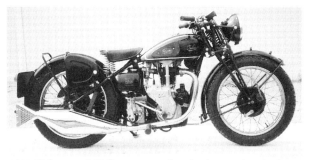

1938 Velocette MAC, 349cc, overhead valve single cylinder.
£2,700–2,900 *BLM*

The MAC, together with the 248cc MOV and 499 MSS were all born in the 1930s, but went on to play a major role in Velocettes post-war success.

> **Don't Forget!**
> *If in doubt please refer to the 'How to Use' section at the beginning of this book.*

l. **1946 Velocette KSS**, 348cc, good condition.
£5,000–5,500 *BLM*

This superb cammy Velo was registered in Devon on the 30th December 1946. It is believed to be the 3rd KSS off the line after WWII. Only 3 owners from new, all in Devon.

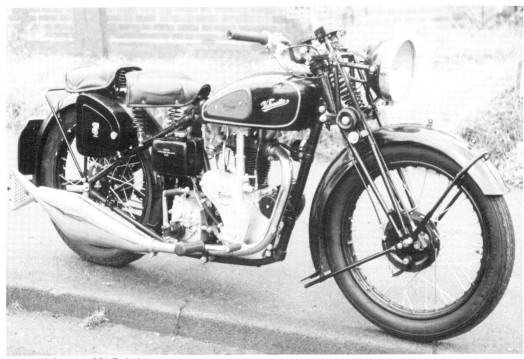

c1946 Velocette MAC, 349cc.
£3,500–3,800 *BKS*

In 1933 Veloce Limited augmented its established range of overhead camshaft models with an overhead valve 250 – the MOV. The newcomer's power unit was a 'high camshaft' design with enclosed valves, and the compact and spritely machine featured a 4-speed gearbox equipped with the company's new footchange mechanism. The following year an overhead valve 350 built along MOV lines appeared. This was the longstroke MAC, which was subsequently bored out to create the 500 MSS. Post-war the trio of overhead valve Velos continued much as before, with rigid frames and Webb girder forks. The MAC gained an alloy cylinder barrel and head for 1951, as well as a telescopic front fork, and was further updated with a swinging arm frame in 1953. The model continued alongside the more sporting 350 Viper until 1960.

1947 Velocette KSS, 348cc, overhead camshaft single, with positive stop, footchange gearbox.
£4,300–4,800 *BKS*

The Velocette factory was renowned for producing high quality single cylinder sports machines. During the 1930s the KSS was the sports machine of the cammy line-up and this particular bike is an excellent example of the model.

The machine was purchased in a dismantled condition by its present owner about 3 years ago and since then has been extensively and expensively restored.
The owner decided to restore the machine to 1948 specification with Dowty front forks, modified petrol tank to accommodate the fork legs and rear wheel drive speedometer. It is fitted with 21in front and 20in rear wheels. The engine was restored by Colin East and the machine has only completed 700 road miles since restoration.

c1950s Velocette Venom, 349cc, overhead valve single cylinder.
£3,000–3,300 *S*

This mchine was constructed from spare parts in the early 1980s. Specification includes fishtail silencer, Woodhead Monroe rear shocks, TT carburettor and non-standard MAC-type front brake.

r. **1954 Velocette LE MkII,** 192cc.
£775–850 *RRN*

Larger capacity than MkI. This particular example has non-standard alloy wheel rims.

1955 Velocette MAC, 349cc, overhead
valve single cylinder, original specification,
concours condition, fully restored.
£2,750–3,000 *BLM*

1956 Velocette LE MkII, 192cc, single valve
water-cooled twin, restoration project, complete
but non-running, ex-Police model.
£280–330 *GAZE*

1959 Velocette Venom, 499cc, overhead valve
single, concours condition, alloy rims, finished
in traditional Velocette black and gold finish.
£3,000–3,500 *Velo*

A 'Thruxtonised' Venom, but in touring mode.

1960 Velocette Viper, 349cc, overhead valve
single cylinder, runs wells, paintwork faded,
non-standard black mudguards, black,
instead of chrome tank finish.
£1,500–1,700 *AT*

1960 Velocette Valiant, 192cc,
overhead valve, flat twin cylinder,
4-speeds, shaft final drive.
£850–1,000 *S*

r. **1961 Velocette Valiant,** 192cc, overhead valve
air-cooled twin, shaft final drive.
£850–1,000 *BKS*

*The Valiant was derived from the famous LE model.
However, it was a far more conventional machine
and employed overhead rather than side valves.*

1961 Velocette Viper, 349cc, good condition.
£2,500–3,000 *BLM*
Traditional British heavyweight single with pushrod-operated valves.

1962 Velocette Venom, 499cc, original condition, lightweight piston and valve gear.
£3,200–3,500 *ELA*

1963 LE Velocette MkIII, 192cc, single valve, water-cooled twin, in running order with MOT, in need of cosmetic restoration.
£380–450 *HOLL*

1965 Velocette MAC, 350cc.
£2,500–2,800 *BLM*
The MAC was first presented to the motorcycling public in the mid-1930s.

1965 Velocette Vogue, 192cc, overhead valve twin, fully enclosed bodywork.
£1,600–1,800 *LEV*

Only 361 Vogues were made. It was one of the sales failures which caused Velocettes collapse a few years later, but because of its rarity the Vogue is now very collectable compared with the LE or even the Valiant.

r. **1967 LE Velocette MkIII,** 192cc, single valve water-cooled twin, original specification, concours condition.
£1,000–1,500 *VER*

VINCENT *(British 1928–56)*

1948 Vincent Rapide Series C, 998cc, V-twin,
84 x 90mm bore and stroke, 45bhp at 5300rpm.
£10,500–11,000 *AT*
First year of Series C Rapide production.

r. **1949 Vincent Comet Series C,** 499cc,
overhead valve single cylinder.
£5,000–5,500 *BKS*

*By removing the rear cylinder from the V-twin
power unit and replacing it with a cast aluminium
frame member, Vincent was able to produce
a 500cc machine of exceptionally high quality.*

1952 Vincent Comet, 499cc, overhead valve
single cylinder, 4-speed, 84 x 90mm bore and
stroke, 28bhp at 5800rpm, unrestored.
£4,500–5,000 *PC*
*Formally on display at a museum in Chelmsford,
Essex, for many years.*

Don't Forget!

*If in doubt please refer to the 'How to Use'
section at the beginning of this book.*

1952 Vincent Series C Comet,
499cc, overhead valve single cylinder.
£4,500–5,000 *VER*

1952 Vincent Comet, 499cc, overhead valve single cylinder, concours, fully restored to new condition.
£5,500–6,000 *PC*

Effectively a Rapide V-twin, minus its rear cylinder, the Series C Comet built from 1948 through to 1954 offered the same degree of refinement as its bigger brother, albeit with reduced performance levels. Even so, the Comet combined a 90mph maximum speed with good fuel economy, and was the ideal touring single for the true enthusiast.

1952 Vincent Black Shadow,
998cc, overhead valve V-twin.
£14,000–14,500 *PM*

Probably Vincent's most famous model, the Black Shadow was essentially a tuned Rapide, giving 55bhp at 5700rpm – some 10 more than the standard model.

1954 Vincent Series C Black Shadow, 998cc, overhead valve 50° V-twin, girdraulic forks, uprated electrical system to 12 volt, Amal Concentric carburettors.
£14,500–15,000 *BKS*

Vincent's mighty Black Shadow could legitimately lay claim to the title of first superbike, both in terms of performance, which at the time of its introduction was greater than virtually anything else on 2 or 4 wheels, and in terms of engineering quality.

l. **1956 Vincent Black Knight Series D,** 998cc.
£11,000–13,000 *VER*

Some 460 Series D models were built, of which 200 were of the enclosed type. This machine was built in 1955 and registered in 1956.

WANDERER
(German 1902–29)

1926 Wanderer V-twin, 800cc, overhead valve narrow angle V-twin, chain final drive.
£14,500–15,000 *WEED*

The Wanderer factory was in Saxony near the DKW (later MZ) works in Zschopau in East Germany.

WOLF *(British 1901–39)*

1922 Wolf Model C 2¾hp, 349cc, 2-speed JAP engine, belt final drive.
£2,500–3,000 *BLM*

Make the most of Miller's

Condition is absolutely vital when assessing the value of a motorcycle. Top class bikes on the whole appreciate much more than less perfect examples. Rare, desirable bikes may command higher prices even when in need of restoration.

YAMAHA *(Japanese 1954–)*

1973 Yamaha RD350, 347cc, piston port, 2-stroke twin cylinder with torque induction, 64 x 54mm bore and stroke, Autolube, 39bhp at 7500rpm, 6-speed, concours condition, fully restored.
£800–1,000 *ARD*

1978 Yamaha SR500, 499cc, 31,000 miles recorded miles, overhead camshaft, single cylinder, 5-speed, disc front brake.
£500–600 *PS*

1979 Yamaha RD250E, 247cc, piston port 2-stroke twin cylinder, front and rear disc brakes.
£750–900 *ARD*

Cast alloy wheels were a feature of the E-Series. Electronic CDI ignition made its first appearance for the 1978 model.

AUTOCYCLES

1923 Propulcycle Autocycle,
99cc, 2-stroke single cylinder engine.
£650–750 *PS*

1933 Excelsior Autocycle, 98cc, Villiers single
cylinder 2-stroke engine, 2-speed gearbox.
£140–150 *BKS*

Locate the Source

*The source of each illustration in
Miller's can be found by checking the
code letters below each caption with the
Key to Illustrations.*

1948 Norman Autocycle, 98cc, requires restoration.
£90–100 *BKS*

*The Norman factory was situated in Ashford, Kent.
The company made its debut at the Earl's Court
Motor Show in 1938 at which they exhibited
2 machines, one of which was a 98cc autocycle known
as the Motobyk. By 1948 this model had changed
very little in design. The engine unit was still a
98cc Villiers 2-stroke underslung unit with power
transmitted to the rear wheel by chain.*

l. **1947 Excelsior Autobyk,** 98cc,
single cylinder 2-stroke engine.
£130–150 *PS*

1947 Raynal Autocycle, 98cc, 2-stroke single cylinder.
£250–300 *NAC*

1949 Cyc Auto Autocycle, 98cc, concours condition.
£550–700 *NAC*

c1950 Power Pak Clip-On Engine, 49cc.
£115–135 *BKS*

*One of the multitude of cycle attachments
that appeared on the market following WWII,
the Power Pak featured a 49cc 2-stroke
engine and was designed to drive the rear
wheel of the bicycle via a roller. The petrol
tank and other ancillary parts were built into
the package to produce a neat installation.*

1949 New Hudson Autocycle, 98cc.
£900–1,100 *BKS*

*New Hudson returned briefly to the manufacture of
2-wheelers in 1940 with the Autocycle. The engine
was Villiers' JDL, and the Autocycle featured pedal
transmission and a rigid front fork. Production
resumed in 1946, by which time New Hudson was
owned by BSA. Post-war developments included the
adoption of pressed-steel blade-type girder forks in
1948, and the Villiers' 2F engine the following year.
Deletion of the 2F power unit brought an end to
Autocycle production in 1958.*

1953 BSA Winged Wheel, 35cc, New Hudson
chassis, Webb, BSA engine, one owner since 1959.
£600–700 *NAC*

1957 New Hudson Autocycle, 98cc,
original, unrestored, some rust.
£475–525 *PS*

l. **1957 New Hudson Autocycle,**
98cc, 2-stroke Villiers engine.
£350–400 *AT*

DIRT BIKES
Pre-1965 Motocross & Trials

At the Classic Scramble, staged as part of the Post TT international race meeting at Mallory Park on Sunday 9 June 1996, over 120 competitors took part in a series of dirt bike races at the Leicestershire circuit. Famous names from the world of off-road racing included the likes of Terry Challinor, Brian Nadin, John Giles, Arthur Browning, Mick Andrews, Chris Horsfield, Ken Sedgeley and Jim Aim. The machines they rode were just as varied and most definitely created an impressive reminder of just what motocross meant three decades or more ago. Amongst the massed ranks of thundering Triumph Metissés, Cheney BSAs, Tribsas, BSA Gold Stars and Victors came a sprinkling of 2-strokes, including CZ twin port, Husqvarna, Cotton, Greeves and Dot machines. The entire sidecar field was made up of Norton Wasp outfits with either 850 or 920cc engines.

All this was a vivid reminder of the great days when the sport was largely known as scrambling – the early post-war period and into the 1950s and early '60s, when most machines were 4-strokes which thumped or popped their way to victory.

It was an age when men were men and a competition Gold Star BSA scrambler was the bike to beat, when riders wore ex-fireman's boots, a rugby jersey or maybe something similar, and fun was fun. Classic scrambling, like classic racing enables competitors and spectators alike to relive those glorious days.

Much the same is also true of Classic pre-1965 trials. Here, too, machines and riders are able to recapture a bygone era. Once again the vast percentage of bikes are of British origin, and with the pre-1965 cut-off, 4-strokes are very much in vogue.

1946 Matchless G80 Rigid Trials, 497cc, overhead valve heavyweight single cylinder.
£2,000–2,250 *BLM*

Between 1946 and early 1955 AMC's (owners of Matchless and AJS) competition models developed from being almost indistinguishable from the normal production roadsters into highly specialised, purpose-built award winners.

1953 BSA ZB32 Gold Star, 348cc.
£1,800–2,000 *BOC*

A hybrid machine assembled using later swinging arm frame, it has been used for various branches of the sport, including grass track and hillclimbing.

l. **1954 Ariel HT5,** 499cc, overhead valve single, ex-works solo motorcycle, 81.8 x 95mm bore and stroke, telescopic forks, swinging arm rear suspension, alloy fuel tank, restored to original specification.
£6,000–6,600 *S*

The Ariel factory in Selly Oak, Birmingham, regularly entered teams of riders, on specially prepared machines, in the year-long season of trade supported trials and scrambles that formed the backbone of British off-road sport throughout the 1940s and 1950s. Overshadowed by the AMC factory in London, with their teams of AJS and Matchless, and the massive effort deployed by BSA – frequently with 2 rider teams – Ariel had the knack of signing up talented young riders, often outriding their competitors from the larger, better budgeted, factories. In 1958 the competition shop at Selly Oak under Clive Bennett, commissioned 3 new machines off the production line, stripped them completely, before rebuilding by hand and issuing the machines as follows: GOV 130 to Ron Langston, GOV 131 to Gordon Blakeway, GOV 132 (now the most famous trials motorcycle in the world) to Sammy Miller. Sammy immediately took it upon himself to lighten GOV 132 with the use of exotic materials, but the sister machines though beautifully prepared, were always ridden in virtually stock specification with the exception of the fitment of lighter hubs taken from the street model Ariel Leader.
Ron Langston confirmed that the trio of Ariels competed in all the main events including the Scottish Six Days, the British Experts and the Scott Trial, winning innumerable Team Prizes and Premier Awards. Due to absorption by BSA into the Small Heath factory, and Ariel's exclusive concentration on twin cylinder 2-strokes, the charismatic Ariel works trials team was disbanded in 1959. This particular machine, GOV 130, went missing for a number of years, and was eventually re-discovered by Bill Lawless, Editor of Trials and Moto Cross News, *a few years ago.*

1957 ESO Scrambler, 498cc, single cylinder, overhead camshaft, unit construction, 4-speed.
£2,500–2,800 *JCZ*

Born in the late 1940s the Czech ESO concern was eventually absorbed into the much larger Jawa company, but not before building a sound reputation for making excellent competition bikes for speedway, motocross and even road racing.

1959 Jawa Six Days S554, 349cc, genuine ex-factory ISDT bike, original specification, concours condition.
£1,800–2,000 *JCZ*

1962 BSA Trials Special, 247cc, originally a C15S Scrambler, modified for trials use, rebuilt, new wheels, alloy rims, shock absorbers, converted to 12 volt electrics.
£800–900 *PS*

1962 BSA Trials C15T, 247cc, overhead valve unit single cylinder.
£1,200–1,500 *BLM*

With its alloy tank, rims, guards, etc, it is virtually a works replica of the type campaigned so successfully by Jeff Smith, Arthur Lampkin and Scott Ellis.

r. 1963 Triumph T20 Trials Cub, 199cc.
£1,200–1,500 *BLM*

By 1962 the over-the-counter trials Cub Works Replica justified the claim. That year's model had the cranked out rear offside sub-frame to allow the exhaust system to at last run inside the frame, heavyweight forks and a wider 4in section rear tyre. By mid-1962 and the ignition points were relocated on the engines timing cover.

> **Miller's is a price GUIDE not a price LIST**

964 Cotton Cobra Special, 247cc, Villiers Starmaker engine, oncours condition, one owner since new, full restoration.
1,600–1,800 *COEC*

he Cotton factory produced both the iron-barrelled standard obra and the alloy Starmaker, known as the Cobra Specials at dditional cost.

1964 Triumph T20 Cub Trials Replica, 199cc, overhead valve single cylinder.
£950–1,100 *PS*

The specification of this particular bike is based on the factory 'works' models of the early/mid-1960s. It was constructed to this specification in 1993 by Headley Cockshott of Otley, West Yorkshire, a long time Cub authority and competitor.

1965 Parilla Wildcat Scrambler, 247cc, high
camshaft single, alloy wheel rims, Ceriani forks,
megaphone exhaust.
£1,600–1,800 *PC*

1969 Ansel Grasstrack Racer, 499cc,
overhead valve JAP engine, AMC gearbox.
£1,000–1,750 *CROW*

1970 Hagon JAP, 499cc, special speedway model.
£1,000–1,750 *CROW*

1965 Sprite Trials, 246cc.
£1,250–1,500 *PC*

*The Birmingham-based Sprite concern was owned
by Frank Hipkin, who built both scrambles and
trials machines during the mid-1960s. Perhaps
Sprite's main claim to fame was Hipkin's brilliant
ploy of not only finding a loophole in the British tax
laws of the day (which allowed motor vehicles in
dismantled or kit form to escape tax), but also to sell
direct to the customer thus cutting out the dealer.
This meant prices were below virtually everyone in
the industry.*

1976 Montesa Cota, 310cc.
£350–450 *PS*

*This machine is a replica of the exact model ridden
by the late Jim Sandiford, the British Montesa
importer. It has had only 2 owners from new.*

l. **1978 Ossa 244 MAR MkIII,** 244cc, 2-stroke
single cylinder, 60 x 72mm bore and stroke, 9:1
compression, 27mm Bing carburettor, Betor forks.
£460–500 *PS*

MILITARY MOTORCYCLES

c1940 Triumph 3HW, 343cc, overhead valve, 70 x 89mm bore and stroke, 6.7:1 compression, 17bhp at 5200rpm, girder forks, rigid frame.
£1,600–1,700 *BLM*
One of the less common War Department bikes.

1940 BSA M20, 496cc, side valve single cylinder, 82 x 94mm bore and stroke, 4.9:1 compression ratio, 13bhp at 4200rpm.
£1,700–1,900 *AT*

The immortal 'British War Bike', everybody's father rode one! The M20 had been part of a new range of singles designed by Val Page when he joined BSA in 1936.

1942 Indian 741B, 499cc, side valve V-twin, 3-speed, girder forks, rigid frame, coil ignition.
£6,000–6,500 *IMC*

1942 Indian 741B, 500cc, side valve V-twin.
£6,000–6,500 *IMC*

A WWII despatch rider's bike in original condition.

l. **1940 Ariel W/NG,** 346cc, overhead valve, 72 x 85mm bore and stroke, 6.5:1 compression, 17bhp at 5800rpm, 4-speed, foot-operated gearbox.
£1,800–2,000 *BLM*

1942 Royal Enfield RE, 126cc, piston port single cylinder 2-stroke, 54 x 55mm, 3-speed, girder forks, rigid frame.
£700–900 *CROW*
Also known as the 'Flying Flea' due to its wartime airborne service.

152 MILITARY MOTORCYCLES

1942 BMW R75 Sidecar, 745cc.
£4,600–5,000 *BKS*

The German armed forces used the BMW R75 combination and its comrade-in-arms, the Zündapp KS750, for many of the tasks that the Willys Jeep performed for the Allies. Inspired by captured FN and Gnome & Rhone outfits, the BMW was equipped with 10 gears comprising 4 ratios in high and low respectively, with a further 2 reverse ratios, driving both the motorcycle's rear wheel and the sidecar's wheel. The result was a machine that was endowed with spectacular off-road abilities, but which was complex and expensive to produce.

1942 Matchless G3L, 348cc, overhead valve single cylinder, 69 x 93mm bore and stroke, 5.9 compression, 4-speed, footchange, telescopic forks, rigid frame, magneto ignition, restored.
£1,400–1,600 *AT*

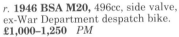

r. **1946 BSA M20,** 496cc, side valve, ex-War Department despatch bike.
£1,000–1,250 *PM*

1942 Harley-Davidson WLC, 748cc, side valve V-twin, 3-speed, coil ignition.
£6,600–7,200 *MVT*

WLC (C stood for Canada – where wartime production was also undertaken).

1942 Harley-Davidson WLA, 748cc, side valve V-twin, 6:1 compression, 23bhp at 4500rpm, 3-speed, coil ignition.
£8,000–8,500 *AT*

US Army machine, fully kitted out.

1964 Triumph TRW, 499cc, side valve vertical twin cylinder, 63 x 80mm bore and stroke, 6:1 compression, 18bhp at 5000rpm, 19in wheels, 4-speed, footchange, magneto ignition.
£1,600–1,800 *BLM*

The TRW was used by several British government departments, including the Royal Air Force.

MONKEY BIKES

1965 Honda CZ100 Monkey Bike,
49cc, overhead valve.
£2,000–2,500 *MAY*

Honda's original Monkey Bike, the CZ100, ran from 1960 through to 1967. The engine produced 4.5bhp at 9500rpm. The gearbox was 3-speed. This particular machine is in concours condition, but missing exhaust guard.

1970 Honda Z50K2, 49.5cc, overhead camshaft, 41.4 x 49.5mm, 2.5bhp at 6000rpm, 3-speed.
£2,600–2,800 *S*

1971 Honda QA50K1, overhead valve, 35.6 x 49.3mm bore and stroke, 1.8bhp at 5000rpm, 2-speed.
£2,400–2,600 *S*

1974 Graziella Foldaway, 49cc, Sachs engine and steering links, 18in (45.5cm) square when folded.
£550–750 *NLM*

Manufactured in Northern Italy in the 1970s by Carnielli, better known for pushbikes. Perhaps too high a quality for commercial success. Fitted with Sachs engine and steering links to aid true compactness, pre-dating Bimota Tesi by several years.

1975 Honda ST70, 71.8cc, overhead camshaft, 47 x 41.4mm bore and stroke, 6bhp at 9000rpm, 3 gears.
£750–950 *BKS*

Fold-up concept, larger than the Monkey Bike which first appeared in 1969.

1975 Honda ST70, 71.8cc, overhead camshaft, horizontal cylinder, only 24 miles from new, concours condition.
£1,800–1,900 *BKS*

1980 Honda Z50R, 49cc.
£670–770 *BKS*

A development of Z50R for off-road use.

MOPEDS

1955 NSU Quickly Moped, 49cc, piston port 2-stroke single cylinder, 40 x 39mm bore and stroke.
£80–100 *BKS*

The Quickly was NSU's most successful design. It first appeared in 1953 and over the course of the next decade a total of 1,111,744 examples were sold all around the world.

1964 NSU Quickly N Moped, 49cc, de luxe version of the best-selling Quickly range.
£200–250 *MAY*

c1972 Motobecane Moped, 49cc.
£5–10 *BKS*

The Motobecane factory commenced production in 1923 and became the largest motorcycle producer in France. The factory recognised that with the French preference for mopeds there was a ready home market and they began to supply this in earnest. The small engined mopeds were sold almost in their millions and by 1972 refinements included even a unique folding 50cc moped for use with the car.

1960 Motom 48S Moped, 49cc, overhead valve, plunger rear suspension, alloy rims.
£400–475 *MAY*

Italian factory (Milan) produced a wide range of models using this engine, even for racing and record breaking.

> **Make the most of Miller's**
>
> *Condition is absolutely vital when assessing the value of a motorcycle. Top class bikes on the whole appreciate much more than less perfect examples. Rare, desirable bikes may command higher prices even when in need of restoration.*

1974 Honda PC50, 49.3cc, overhead valve, single speed, 42 x 35.6mm, 1.8bhp at 5700rpm.
£115–125 *BKS*

Launched in 1969, the PC50 became one of Honda's most successful ultra-lightweights during the early 1970s.

RACING BIKES

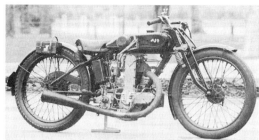

1928 AJS K10, 495cc, overhead camshaft, stored for 30 years, original condition, matching frame, engine and gearbox numbers, 3-speed close-ratio unit, recently rebuilt, new clutch, TT-type fuel tank, new bearings, piston, valves, Druid front fork overhauled, new bushes, spindles and springs.
£10,500–12,000 *BKS*

Originally manufacturers of proprietary engines, the Stevens brothers introduced the first AJS motorcycle in 1911. The first AJS machines were side valve engined lightweights offered with belt-drive transmission or optional all-chain drive with 2-speed countershaft gearbox. This latter feature enabled them to put up a good showing in the Isle of Man TT's new Junior Class, an event AJS would later dominate. Eric Williams scored the marque's maiden Junior TT victory in 1914, and the first post-war Junior event saw the new overhead valve AJS in commanding form. Indeed, so good was the newcomer that Howard Davies rode it to a unique double victory the following year, winning both the Junior and Senior TTs.

In 1927 the works 350cc racers appeared with a new overhead camshaft engine. The camshaft was chain driven, its distinctive cast alloy case extending forwards to the front-mounted magneto. A catalogued model from 1928, the cammy AJS was built in 350 and 500cc capacities initially. A 250cc version followed, Jimmy Guthrie winning the Lightweight TT on one in 1930. Production ceased with the Matchless takeover in 1931.

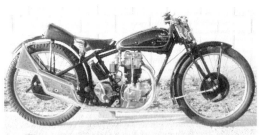

1930 Rudge Racer, 499cc, 4 valve twin port single cylinder, Brooklands 'can' exhausts.
£4,000–4,500 *BLM*

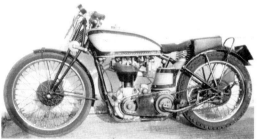

1936 Norton Manx Style Racer, single overhead camshaft, alloy petrol and oil tanks, Brooklands exhaust.
£5,000–5,750 *AT*

1936 AJS R7, 349cc, single overhead camshaft, hairpin valve springs, footchange gearbox.
£7,000–8,000 *PC*

AJS introduced their original R7 over-the-counter racer in 1930. Produced throughout most of the 1930s it was the forerunner of its much more famous post-war 7R 'Boy Racer'. Although it proved popular with clubmen, it never achieved the success of its inter-war years rivals, the KTT Velocette and overhead camshaft Norton.

1950 MV Agusta 125 Racer, 123.5cc, piston port, single cylinder 2-stroke, 4-speed close-ratio gearbox, blade forks, swinging arm rear suspension, with shock absorbers and friction damping.
£3,800–4,200 *PC*

MV began with 2-strokes for both road and track. Now very rare. This example is extremely original.

1954 MV Agusta Competizione Racer, 124cc, single overhead camshaft.
£10,000–11,000 *PC*

This machine is the single overhead camshaft version of the factory's double overhead camshaft 125 racer. Built for sale to customers – at the time it cost more than a 1000cc Vincent Black Shadow! Mike Hailwood had his first ever race on just such a model at Oulton Park in 1957.

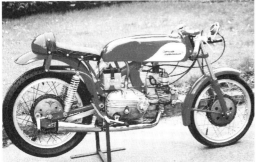

1962 Aermacchi Ala D'Oro, 246cc, overhead valve, 66 x 72mm bore and stroke, long-stroke, wet clutch, 4-speed, 30mm carburettor, DS5 camshaft, 10mm Stellite tappets, 9200rpm.
£5,500–6,000 *PC*

1971 Triumph Ex-Works Production Racer 'Slippery Sam', 749cc, 3 cylinders, overhead valve, 11.5:1 compression, 3 Amal Concentric 27mm carburettors, 72/75 bhp at 8500rpm, double disc front brake.
£100,000+ *TRI*

This machine was winner of a record breaking 5 TTs in subsequent years: Ray Pickerell (1971 & 1972), Tony Jefferies (1973), Mick Grant (1974) and finally Dave Croxford/Alex George (1975). Currently stored in the National Motorcycle Museum.

1974 Isle of Man TT Production Race class winners:
750cc	*Mick Grant – Triumph Trident (10)*
500cc	*Keith Martin – Kawasaki (47)*
250cc	*Martin Sharpe – Yamaha (67)*

Locate the Source
The source of each illustration in Miller's can be found by checking the code letters below each caption with the Key to Illustrations.

1962 Benelli Racer, 49cc, piston port, 2-stroke, 4-speed hand-operated twistgrip gearchange, 4bhp, 67mph maximum speed.
£4,600–5,200 *S*

Actual machine ridden by Ralph Bryans to 15th place in the very first Isle of Man 50cc TT in June 1962 – at a race average speed of just under 59mph. Subject to a comprehensive rebuild by enthusiast Robin Read in 1985.

1970 Weslake NRE Racing Sidecar, 888cc, Windrick chassis, NRE engine, Quaife 4-speed close-ratio gearbox, fitted in Norton Commando box, 16in (40.5cm) front spoke wheel with single disc brakes, rear and sidecar both Mini wheels, Dunlop CR65 tyres.
£10,000–12,000 *PC*

Currently raced by Raymond Reeves and John Marshall who have won the British Classic Motorcycle Racing Club Sidecar Championship 3 times in 1993, 1995 and 1996.

r. **c1975 Harley Davidson RR500,** 494cc, 4 carburettors, 66.7 x 70mm bore and stroke, double disc front brake, drum rear brakes.
£11,000–12,000 *AtMC*

Ex-factory development machine.

FORGOTTEN ERA RACING

As everyone knows, time marches on, and ideas that once started as brave new ways forward eventually become dinosaurs to the next generation who grow up with a different philosophy.

The beauty of this endless cycle, however, is that there is always room to accommodate everyone. Take road racing for example. First it was the Vintage Motor Cycle Club who froze out the later classics in order to form a competitive environment for the earlier machines. Enter the Classic Racing Motorcycle Club which initially did the same in outlawing the Oriental breeds that killed off the British racing single. Then, ten years ago, a gentleman by the name of Mick Newton and a bunch of like-minded pals got together and decided it was high time someone catered for those machines in no-man's land – the Japanese era bikes that were no longer competitive in the ever advancing technology of modern racing, yet were ineligible to race with the Historic clubs.

Two of the club's founder members are still the men to beat – Graham Salter (47) on the ex-Graeme Crosby Moriwaki and Dave Brown (46) P&M 1000.
Forgotten Era Club Solo Racing, Cadwell Park, 1997.

They persuaded the Retford and District Club to give them grid space at one of their meetings and the Forgotten Racing Club (FRC) was born. From then on it blossomed and more classes opened to accommodate the machinery coming out from enforced retirement. Currently the FRC Championship rounds run within the programmes of Grantham Pegasus and Darley Moor clubs. Production-based race machines from

1963–76 such as the RD Yamaha, CB Honda and GT Suzuki can be found in the Forgotten Era class, which covers all capacities from 125 through to 1000cc along with early race ware in the form of the TR Yamaha, MT Honda etc. The Factory class covers pukka factory-built race machines up to 1987 such as the TZ Yamaha in its varying capacities and forms (ie Maxton, Spondon, Seeley etc) RG Suzuki, Cotton and the various Rotax-based offsprings, Armstrong etc, GP specials of the period like the 500cc 3 cylinder Yamaha-based Zegers and awesome 4-stroke Formula 1 machines of Moriwaki, Yoshimura, Harris and P&M. The beauty of the classes is that often one bike is eligible for both FE and Factory.

Steve Kirk/Keith Johnson (2), Andy/Jake Beckworth (6), Derek Morgan/Paul Burke(17) – all GS1000 Suzukis. Ian Waugh/Andy Baldock – 1000cc Puma Twin (10).
Forgotten Era Sidecar Racing, Cadwell Park, 1997.

The club is not solely the domain of the Japanese, however, for there is a good smattering of Norton, Triumph and BSA in there too. Sidecars are handsomely catered for also, with twin and multi-cylinder classes from T140 Triumphs and 1000cc Pumas to GS1000 based Suzukis, the mighty Laverda Jota and even a unique Barton Phoenix 750cc square four. The success of the club and the guaranteed grids has enabled them to stage races at the major national meetings, the Post TT at Mallory Park and Scarborough's Gold Cup being prime examples. Presently the club enjoys backing from a host of sponsors which means that riders can benefit from not only product support but actual prize money too, and that includes each and every class. Not bad for an upstart of only ten years. So, if you fancy a whirl on that old bike at anything up to 13 meetings at many of the country's top circuits, membership of the FRC is £20 per annum and a full starter pack with details and regulations is available from Mrs Chris Pinches, 73 High Street, Morton, Bourne, Lincs. PE10 ONR. Tel: 01778 570535.

Nigel Clark

l. **1970s Zegers,** 500cc, 3 cylinder Yamaha based machine, 2-stroke.
Est. £2,800–3,000 *FRC*
This is the machine used by Carl Portwood.

1971 Yamsel Racer, 347cc, engine overhauled.
£2,900–3,200 *BKS*

Japanese 2-strokes – particularly Yamahas – had dominated the Lightweight and Junior classes at national level by the early 1970s. Although the Oriental strokers had power in abundance, their handling often left plenty to be desired. European frame builders were quick to step in, and in Britain Colin Seeley found plenty of takers for his beautifully-engineered Yamsels. One of the first to successfully exploit the Yamaha-powered Seeley was John Cooper, whose 250 and 350 Yamsels were the bikes to beat for many years. Rolling chassis number CS1837S was delivered to Screen & Plastics Ltd, of Birmingham, in August 1971. At present it is fitted with a 1977 Yamaha TZ250D engine converted to TZ350 specification. The engine has been overhauled by renowned motorcycle race engineer Dave Hickman, and has completed approximately 8 trouble-free laps of Silverstone (Classic Festival, May 1996) since re-installation. This machine has letters of authentication from Colin Seeley and Yamaha, plus a CRMC registration certificate.

1977 Honda CB400F Formula 3 Racer, 398cc, single overhead camshaft, 4 cylinders, modifications to bring it up to race standard include transistorised ignition, conversion to chain primary drive, reinforced drive cushions, HRC short stroke crankshaft, full race camshaft, racing exhaust, rear sets and an alloy petrol tank, seat and wheel rims.
£4,000–4,500 *BKS*

This historic machine was originally raced by Nettleton Motorcycles, with John Kidson in the saddle, during the 1977 Formula 3 World Championship, securing a victory in the Formula 3 race at the TT and taking the championship overall.

The following year, now piloted by Tony Rutter, it achieved a 4th place in the TT, 6th at the Ulster Grand Prix and 4th overall in the championship. It was subsequently retired from racing, and was acquired by the present owner in 1980.

Modifications for racing to include a reduction in capacity to 398cc achieved by fitting the Japanese home market barrels, in place of the 403cc export market barrels in order to comply with the championship regulations, an HRC short stroke crankshaft, full race camshaft, racing exhaust, rear sets, alloy petrol tank, seat and wheel rims.

1976 Yamaha TZ350, 347.4cc, 2-stroke, water-cooled, 6-speed, 64 x 54mm bore and stroke, 60bhp at 10,000rpm.
£2,600–3,200 *FRC*

World Superbike Honda boss, Neil Tuxworth on Bob Heath's TZ350 Yamaha.

r. **1981 Suzuki RG500 MkVI,**
494.69cc, square four 2-stroke.
£5,500–6,000 *FRC*

Ex-Chris Martin, Phil Riley (purchased new in Holland). Now raced by Tony Plumridge in Forgotten Era events. Maintained from new by Roger Keen. Still winning races today. One of the very best examples in existence.

SCOOTERS

1953 Douglas Vespa Model G, 125cc, single cylinder, 2-stroke, 56.5 x 49.8mm bore and stroke.
£860–940 *BKS*

In 1948 Douglas boss, Claude McCormack, vacationing in Italy, was amazed by the number of Vespa scooters he saw on the streets, and so came about a tie-up between makers Piaggio, and the long established Bristol-based concern. Douglas launched its Vespa range on 15th March 1951, going on to construct a total of 126,230 licence-built Vespa's over the next 20 years.

1949 Brockhouse Corgi, 98cc, Excelsior Spryt 2-stroke engine, 50 x 50mm bore and stroke.
£1,400–1,600 *ELA*

This machine was manufactured by Brockhouse Engineering and was based on the Welbike, a lightweight foldable paratrooper scooter built by Excelsior during WWII.

Don't Forget!

If in doubt please refer to the 'How to Use' section at the beginning of this book.

r. **1961 Vespa GS160,** 160cc.
£1,600–1,800 *MAY*

The larger engined GS160 was built from 1962 through to 1964. Both the bore and stroke were enlarged – 58 x 60mm – providing 8.2bhp at 6,500rpm via a Dell'Orto S1 27/23 for a maximum speed of 65mph.

SIDECARS

c1920 Royal Enfield 8hp Combination,
finished in two-tone green, complete with sidecar
screen, wicker basket, petrol can and trailer.
£6,200–6,800 *BKS*

*Like many other British motorcycle
manufacturers, Royal Enfield's origins were in the
bicycle trade. The Redditch company built its first
powered vehicles, De Dion-engined tricycles and
quadricycles, in the closing years of the 19th
century, and its first motorcycle around 1900.
By 1904 the firm was concentrating on car
production, resuming motorcycle manufacture in
1910 with a Motosacoche-powered lightweight.
Two years later came the successful 6hp
motorcycle combination, with JAP V-twin engine,
2-speed gear, and all chain drive. Enfield's
characteristic cush-drive rear hub appeared for
the first time on this model. When motorcycle
production resumed after WWI, the Enfield
combination re-appeared with an 8hp JAP engine.*

1923 Triumph S.D. Combination, 550cc.
£4,600–5,000 *BKS*

*The arrival of the 1920s saw the period when
Triumph finally left belt drive behind and entered
the era of chain drive and internal expanding brakes.
The famous Model H which saw sterling service
during the Great War began to be updated and this
gradually saw the introduction of the S.D. Model.
Introduced in 1920 the machine was fitted with all
chain drive, a 3-speed gearbox of Triumph design
and a multi-plate clutch with a shock absorber
mounted on an extension to the gearbox mainshaft.
This feature was called the spring drive and hence
the name S.D. was adopted for the new 550cc model.
This new machine was ideally suited at the time
for use with a sidecar and it became a popular
combination, especially when fitted with Triumph's
own Gloria sidecar.*

1926 Coventry Eagle and Sidecar,
998cc, JAP V-twin engine.
£14,000–16,000 *VER*

> **Miller's is a price GUIDE
> not a price LIST**

r. **1927 AJS and Sidecar,** 346cc.
£4,500–5,000 *VER*

1929 Matchless XR2 with Sidecar, 998cc, V-twin, hand change.
£6,000–7,000 *AMOC*

1950 Vincent Black Shadow with Steib Sidecar, 998cc.
£17,000–18,500 *BKS*

Although a limited number of Brampton forked B series Black Shadows were produced following the introduction of the model in 1949, the majority of Vincent's new 125mph masterpieces were produced to the C Series specification and therefore benefited from being fitted with Vincent's Girdraulic front forks.

The 15mph superiority in performance that the Black Shadow had over its nearest rival and progenitor, the Rapide, was achieved by increasing the carburettor bore six from the Rapide's 1⅟₁₆in to 1⅛in and raising the compression ratio from 6.45:1 to 7.3:1. These measures, along with careful engine assembly and preparation at the Stevenage works resulted in a power gain of 10bhp for the new model.

The only noticeable external difference between the 2 models was the baked-on new finish of the Black Shadow's engine cases, cylinders and heads.

1959 BSA A7 Gold Flash with Watsonian Child/Adult Sidecar, 497cc, overhead valve twin, Siamesed exhaust, full width brake hubs.
£2,500–3,000 *VER*

1930 Norton Model 19 Special with Swallow Sidecar, 588cc, Zeppelin-style single seat sidecar, special equipment includes studded rear type competition twist grip, dyno, TT fast change, large tanks and special tune dry sump.
£6,800–7,400 *BKS*

The prototype dry sump suggests that this may have been a works development model and records of this bike are held at the Science Museum, London. It was at one time owned by the Duke of Hamilton.

1955 BSA M21 with Double Adult Sidecar, 596cc, side valve, telescopic forks, rigid frame, standard used condition, unrestored.
£1,300–1,500 *BMM*

1958 Ariel Square Four MkII with Watsonian Sidecar, 995cc, overhead valve square four.
£6,000–7,000 *CCR*

For 1954 the only real change for the year was to an SU carburettor which necessitated a frame modification and to the inlet tract. Compared with the MkI, the MkII featured 4 exhaust pipes, instead of the 2. Another feature of that year's machine was the use of a sport front mudguard.

r. 1965 Gemini Double Adult Sidecar, one of the favourite double adult sidecars.
£250–300 *BKS*

SPECIALS

1939/58 Velocette KSS/Venom Special, 348cc.
£2,100–2,300 *BKS*

*This machine was constructed some 3 decades ago –
based on a 1958 Venom swinging arm frame and
a 1939 KSS overhead camshaft engine.
It subsequently spent most of its life taking part in
various racing events, now in road trim.*

**1960/1997 Dresda Triton
Replica,** 744cc, Triumph T140E
unit engine, 76 x 82mm bore and
stroke, 5-speed, Manx Norton-type
frame, Roadholder forks.
£3,500–4,000 *OxM*

*Built mainly from new
components. Ex-racer Dave Degens
has been building specials for the
last 30 years.*

r. **c1961 Velocette Voletta
Special,** 192cc.
£1,300–1,500 *NDB*

*This unique machine was built and
registered in 1961 by BMG
Motorcycles (makers of the
Desmodromic valve gear for Velocette
singles) of Ilford, Essex. The original
idea was to build a production batch,
but this never happened. The bike
uses a water-cooled LE MkIII engine
mounted in a modified Valiant
chassis. At one time it is believed
that a full size 250cc engine was
built, but this has proved untraceable.*

1957 Triton Special, 749cc, pre-unit Triumph
engine in Norton Dominator wideline frame.
£2,800–3,000 *AT*

*A most interesting bike – rebuilt from new parts –
wideline frame (Norton) with pre-unit Triumph
converted to 750cc.*

1958 Triton Special, 750cc, wideline frame, BSA
wheels, TLS front brake, T110 pre-unit engine with
Morgo big-bore conversion, including barrels and
9-stud cylinder head, BSA gearbox, primary cases,
alloy fuel and oil tanks.
£3,600–3,800 *BLM*

Miller's is a price GUIDE
not a price LIST

---

l. **1967 AJS Model 20 Special,**
497cc, alloy competition fuel tank,
alloy central oil tank, alloy side
panels, hi-level exhaust, fork
gaiters, single seat, alloy guards.
£4,000–4,500 *BLM*

*Built using mainly AMC components
this enduro-type machine is,
however, very much a special.*

1969 Jawa/Norton Special, 499cc, double overhead camshaft, Norton 99 wideline Featherbed chassis with Norton forks and wheels, excellent condition.
£1,500–1,800 *BMM*

c1970 Vincent Egli-Shadow Spec, 998cc, Fritz Egli chassis, Ceriani front forks, Yamaha TD/TR 4LS front brake.
£14,000–15,000 *AtMC*

c1955/70 Egli-Vincent, 998cc, fitted with late Series D Black Shadow engine, built into Eric Cheney frame by Roger Slater in 1970, Grimeca brakes and M.P. forks.
£8,300–9,300 *BKS*

Swiss engineer, Fritz Egli, saw the continuing potential of Vincent's 998cc V-twin engine in competition several years after Vincent production ceased in 1955 and designed his all new frame into which he shoe-horned the V-twin unit.

1972 Triton 3 cylinder, 740cc, Triumph/BSA engine mounted in Norton Featherbed chassis, Roadholder forks, Manx rear wheel, Italian Oldani front wheel, incomplete, in need of restoration.
£1,300–1,500 *BKS*

1976 Rickman/Kawasaki 900CR, 903cc, double overhead camshaft air-cooled four, double loop chassis, 4 pipe exhaust, triple disc brakes, cast alloy wheels.
£3,800–4,100 *PC*

The Rickman brothers, Don and Derek, of New Milton, Hants, offered the Rickman/Kawasaki 903cc Z1 in various guises, but the café racer (CR) was the most popular. This turned a stock Z1 into a sleek sportster with its racer-style looks, incredible 130mph plus performance and excellent handling, it was one of the most exciting street bikes of the mid-1970s.

1978 Harris/Kawasaki Z900 Special, 903cc, Kawasaki double overhead camshaft 4 cylinder-engined special.
£3,900–4,300 *PC*

This bike was built in only very small numbers.

l. **1979 Harris-Kawasaki Magnum 1,** 1260cc, double overhead camshaft, 4 cylinder, monoshock chassis, 5-spoke cast alloy wheels, triple disc brakes, supercharged special producing 125bhp.
£3,300–3,600 *PC*

MEMORABILIA
Badges

A Grasshopper MCC badge,
Chingford, 1950s,
3in (7.5cm) wide.
£18–20 ATF

**A Sunbeam Owners'
Fellowship badge,** c1960,
2½in (6.5cm) diam.
£20–22 ATF

Books & Brochures

The Motor Cycle, No. 7, Vol 1,
Wednesday May 13th 1903,
11 x 8½in (28 x 21.5cm).
£18–20 DM

l. Motor Cycling Manual, 5th
edition, 1920, 7 x 5in (18 x 12.5cm).
£22–25 DM

The Douglas Dirt Track Machine,
Douglas Motor Cycles brochure,
c1930, 9½ x 6¼in (24 x 16cm).
£40–45 PC

l. The Excelsior Dirt Track Speedway Machine
leaflet, 1.11.48, 11½ x 8½in (29 x 21.5cm).
£18–20 PC

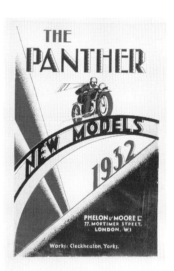

**The Panther, New
Models** brochure, 1932,
9½ x 6½in (24 x 16.5cm).
£12–15 DM

Posters

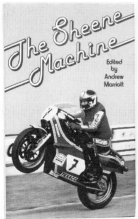

The Sheene Machine,
edited by Andrew Marriott,
1979, 9 x 5½in (23 x 14cm).
£10–12 DM

**A Moto Gilera two
colour poster,** 1951,
and an MV calendar.
£185–200 BKS

An AJS advertising poster,
framed and glazed, c1949.
£160–180 BKS

Signs

A Triumph Motors & Cycles enamel sign, c1920, 45¼ x 60¼in (115 x 153cm). **£200–250** *CRC*

An AA Motor Cycle Specialist hanging enamel sign, c1920, 31 x 22in (79 x 56cm). **£350–375** *JUN*

A Shell Motor Oil enamel advertising sign in the shape of a gallon can, c1920, 20 x 16in (51 x 40.5cm). **£300–350** *JUN*

Pump Globes

l. **A Power Regular glass petrol pump globe,** c1950, 19in (48.5cm) high. **£180–200** *JUN*

r. **A Shell Economy glass petrol pump globe,** 1950s. **£180–200** *JUN*

Miscellaneous

A BSA tool kit, in a leather case, 1920s. **£25–30** *ATF*

r. **A klaxon horn,** late 1920–30s. **£80–90** *ATF*

A Kellermann clockwork despatch rider, c1930, 6in (15cm) long. **£150–175** *RAR*

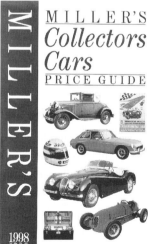

167

GLOSSARY

We have attempted to define some of the terms that you will come across in this book. If there are any other terms or technicalities you would like explained or you feel should be included in future editions, please let us know.

ACU – Auto Cycle Union, who control a large part of British motorcycle sport.

Advanced ignition – Ignition timing set causing firing before the piston reaches centre top, variation is now automatic.

Air-cooling – Most motorcycles rely on air-cooling to the atmosphere.

Air intake – The carburettor port admitting air to mix with fuel from the float chamber.

AMCA – Amateur Motor Cycle Association, promoters of English off-road events.

APMC – The Association of Pioneer Motor Cyclists.

Auto Cycle Club – Formed in 1903 it was the original governing body of motorcycle sport, in 1907 became the Auto Cycle Union.

Automatic inlet valve – Activated by the engine suction. Forerunner of the mechanically operated valve.

Balloon tyres – Wide section, low pressure, soft running tyres, used on tourers for comfort.

Beaded-edge tyres – Encased rubber beads in channel on wheel rim.

Belt drive – A leather or fabric belt from engine or gearbox to rear wheel.

BHP – A measure of engine output, eg to lift 33,000lb one foot in a minute requires one horsepower.

BMCRC – British Motor Cycle Racing Club, formed in 1909.

BMF – British Motorcycle Federation.

Bore/stroke ratio – Cylinder diameter ratio to stroke.

Cam – Device for opening and closing a valve.

Camshaft – The mounting shaft for the cam, can be in low, high or overhead position.

Carburettor – Used to produce the air/fuel mixture.

Chain drive – Primary form of drive from engine to gearbox and secondary gearbox to rear wheel.

Combustion chamber – Area where the fuel/air mixture is compressed and fired, between piston and cylinder head.

Compression ratio – The fuel/air mixture compression degree.

Crankcase – The casing enclosing the crankshaft and its attachments.

Crankshaft – The shaft for converting the up-and-down piston motion into rotary.

Cylinder – Containing the piston and capped by the cylinder head, is the site of the explosion which provides power.

Cylinder head – In a vertical engine caps off the top end of the cylinder. In a 4-stroke engine carries the valves.

Damper – Used for slowing down movement in suspension system or as crankshaft balance.

Displacement – The engine capacity or amount of volume displaced by the movement of the piston from bottom dead centre to top dead centre.

Distributor – A gear driven contact sending high tension current to spark plugs.

DOHC – Double overhead camshaft.

Dry sump – Two oil pumps, one supplying oil to the bearings from a tank, the other to return it to the tank.

Earles forks – An unusual front fork design. A long leading link and rigid pivot through both links behind the wheel.

Featherbed – A Norton frame, designed by Rex and Crommie McCandless, Belfast, used for racing machines from 1950, road machines from 1953.

FIM – Federation Internationale Motorcycliste, controls motorcycle sport worldwide.

Flat head – A flat surfaced cylinder head.

Flat twin – An engine with 2 horizontally opposed cylinders, or 4 to make a Flat Four.

Float – A plastic or brass box which floats upon the fuel in a float chamber and operates the needle valve controlling the fuel.

Flywheel – Attached to the crankshaft this heavy wheel smooths intermittent firing impulses and helps slow running.

Friction drive – An early form of drive using discs in contact instead of chains and gears.

Gearbox – Cased trains of pinion wheels which can be moved to provide alternative ratios.

Gear ratios – Differential rates of speed between sets of pinions to provide higher or lower rotation of the rear wheel in relation to the engine.

GP – Grand Prix, an international race to a fixed formula.

High camshaft – Mounted high up on the engine to shorten the pushrods in an ohv formation.

IOE – Inlet over exhaust, a common arrangement with an overhead inlet and side exhaust.

Leaf spring – Metal blades clamped and bolted together, used in suspension many years ago.

Magneto – A high tension dynamo producing current for the ignition spark. Superseded by coil ignition.

Main bearings – Bearings in which the crankshaft runs.

Manifold – Collection of pipes supplying mixture or taking away fumes.

MCC – The Motor Cycling club which runs sporting events. Formed in 1902.

Moped – A light motorcycle of under 50cc with pedals attached.

OHC – Overhead camshaft, can be either single or double.

OHV – Overhead valve engine.

Overhead cam – An engine with overhead camshaft or camshafts operating its valves.

Overhead valve – A valve mounted in the cylinder head.

Pinking – A distinctive noise from an engine with over-advanced ignition or inferior fuel.

Piston – The component driven down the cylinder by expanding gases.

Post-vintage – A motorcycle made after December 31, 1930 and before January 1, 1945.

Pressure plate – The plate against which the clutch springs react to load the friction plates.

Pushrods – Operating rods for overhead valves, working from cams below the cylinder.

Rotary valve – A valve driven from the camshaft for inlet or exhaust and usually a disc or cylinder shape. For either 2-or 4-stroke engines.

SACU – Scottish Auto Cycle Union, which controls motorcyle sport in Scotland.

SAE – Society of Automotive Engineers. Used in a system of classifying engine oils such as SAE30, IOW/50 etc.

Shock absorber – A damper, used to control up-and-down movement of suspension or to cushion a drive train.

Silencer – Device fitted to the exhaust system of an engine whereby the pressure of the exhaust gases is considerably reduced before reaching the outer air.

Swinging arm – Rear suspension by radius arms carrying the wheel and attached to the frame at the other end.

Torque – Twisting rotational force in a shaft, can be measured to show at what point an engine develops most torque.

INDEX TO ADVERTISERS

BIBLIOGRAPHY

Bacon, Roy; British Motorcycles of the 1930s, Osprey, 1986
Bacon, Roy; Matchless & AJS Restoration, Osprey, 1993
Bacon, Roy; Norton Twin Restoration, Osprey, 1993
Bacon Roy; Triumph Twins & Triples, Osprey, 1990
Birkitt Malcolm; Harley-Davidson, Osprey, 1993
Champ, Robert Cordon; Sunbeam S7/S8 Super Profile, Haynes, 1983
Davis, Ivor; It's a Triumph, Haynes, 1980
Morley Don; and Woolett, Mick; Classic Motorcycles, BMW, Osprey, 1992
Morley, Don; Classic Motorcycles, Triumph, Osprey, 1991
Stuart, Garry; and Carroll, John; Classic Motorcycles, Indian, Osprey, 1994
Tragatsch, Erwin, ed; The New Illustrated Encyclopedia of Motorcycles, Grange Books, 1993

Walker, Mick; Aermacchi, Transport Source Books, 1995
Walker, Mick; Benelli, Transport Source Books, 1996
Walker, Mick; BMW Twins Restoration, Osprey, 1992
Walker, Mick, and Carrick, Rob;
British Performance 2-strokes, Transport Source Books, 1997
Walker, Mick; Ducati Singles, Osprey 1997
Walker, Mick; Hamlyn History of Motorcycling, Hamlyn, 1997
Walker, Mick; Morini, Transport Source Books, 1996
Walker, Mick; MZ, Transport Source Books, 1996
Wherrett, Duncan; Classic Motorcycles, Vincent, Osprey, 1994
Woollett, Mick; Norton, Osprey, 1992

DIRECTORY OF MUSEUMS

Battlesbridge Motorcycle Museum
Muggeridge Farm, Maltings Road,
Battlesbridge, SS11 7RF
Tel: 01268 769392/560866
An interesting collection of classic motorcycles & scooters
in a small informal 'museum'. Open Sundays 10.30am -
4pm. Adults £1, children free.

Birmingham Museum of Science & Industry
136 Newhall Street, Birmingham, B3 1RZ
Tel: 0121 235 1651
A small collection of motorcycles right in the heart of the
city. Open Monday to Saturday 9.30am-5pm. Sunday
2pm-5pm. Closed December 25-26, and January 1.
Admission free.

Bristol Industrial Museum
Princes Wharf, City Docks, Bristol, BS1 4RN
Tel: 0117 925 1470
A small collection of Bristol-made Douglas machines,
including the only surviving V4 of 1908. There is also a
1972 Quasar. Open Saturday to Wednesday 10am-1pm
and 2pm-5pm. Closed Thursdays and Fridays, also
Good Friday, December 25-27 and January 1. Adults £2,
under 16s free.

Brooklands Museum
The Clubhouse, Brooklands Road, Weybridge, KT13 0QN
Tel: 01932 857381
The birthplace of British motorsport and aviation,
Brooklands has several motorcycles on display. Open
Saturday and Sunday 10am-4pm. Guided tours at 10.30am
and 2pm on Tuesdays, Wednesdays and Thursdays.
Adults £4, OAPs and students £3, children £2.

Cotton's Classic Bikes, Phil
Victoria Road Museum, Ulverston, LA12 0BY
Tel: 01229 586099
Working Museum where most of the exhibits are available
to buy.
Open 10am to 4.30pm Tuesday - Saturday, closed Sunday
& Monday.

Craven Collection of Classic Motorcycles
Brockfield Villa, Stockton-on-the-Forest, YO3 9UE
Tel: 01904 488461/400493
A private collection of over 180 Vintage & Post-War
Classic Motorcycles.
Open to the public on first Sunday of every month and
Bank Holiday Mondays, 10am-4pm.
Club visits & private parties arranged.
Admission: Adults £2.00, Children under 10 years Free.

Foulkes-Halbard of Filching
Filching Manor, Jevington Road, Wannock, Polegate,
BN26 5QA
Tel: 01323 487838
A collection of 30 motorcycles, including pre-'40s American
bikes ex-Steve McQueen, as well as 100 cars dating from
1893-1993. Open 7 days a week in summer 10.30-4.30pm.
Thurs-Sunday in winter, or by appointment. Adults £3,
OAPs and children £2.

Grampian Transport Museum
Main Street, Alford, Aberdeenshire, AB33 8AD
Tel: 019755 62292
A collection of 30-40 machines ranging from a 1902
Beeston Humber to a Norton F1. Mods and Rockers caff
display with Triton and Triumph Tina scooter.
Competition section includes 1913 Indian twin and 1976
Rob North replica Trident racer. Open March 28-October
31, 10am-5pm. Adults £2.30, children 80p, OAPs £1.50,
family ticket £5.

Haynes Sparkford Motor Museum
Sparkford, Yeovil, BA22 7LH
Tel: 01963 440804
Collection of 30 plus machines from a 1914 BSA onwards.
Video theatre. Bookshop. Open Monday to Sunday
9.30am-5.30pm. Closed December 25-26 and January 1.
Adults £4.50, OAPs £4, children £2.75.

Miller Museum, Sammy
Gore Road, New Milton, BH25 6TF
Tel: 01425 619696
Sammy Miller is a living legend in the world of motorcycle
racing, and what started out as a hobby 30 years ago has
become a collection of what is arguably the best selection of
competition motorcycles in the country. The museum was
opened in 1983 by John Surtees and is much more than a
static collection. All bikes are in working order and
wherever possible are run in classic bike events
throughout the year. Many of the racing bikes are still
fully competitive. At present there are 200 bikes in the

Museum, many of them extremely rare. New exhibits are
being sought all the time to add to the collection, with
much of the restoration work being carried out on the
premises by Sammy Miller himself. There are interesting
artefacts and items of memorabilia connected to the
motorcycling world on display, including many cups and
trophies won by Sammy over the years. A typical
motorcycle workshop of 1925 has been reconstructed,
showing a large display of the tools used at that time.
Open 10.30am-4.30pm every day, April-October 10.30am-
4.30pm Sats and Suns, November-March. The museum is
situated 15 miles west of Southampton and 10 miles east
of Bournemouth at New Milton, Hants.

Mouldsworth Motor Museum
Smithy Lane, Mouldsworth, Chester, CH3 8AR
Tel: 01928 731781

Murray's Motorcycle Museum
Bungalow Corner, TT Course, Isle of Man.
Tel: 01624 861719
Collection of 140 machines, including Hailwood's 250cc
Mondial and Honda 125cc and the amazing 500cc
4 cylinder roadster designed by John Wooler. Open May to
September 10am-5pm. Adults £2, OAPs and children £1.

Museum of British Road Transport
St. Agnes Lane, Hales Street, Coventry, CV1 1PN.
Tel: 01203 832425
Collection includes 65 motorcycles, with local firms such as
Coventry Eagle, Coventry Victor, Francis-Barnett,
Triumph and Rudge well represented. Close to city centre.
Open every day except December 24-26, 10am-5pm.
Adults £2.50, children, OAPs and unemployed £1.50.

Museum of Transport
Kelvin Hall, 1 Bunhouse Road, Glasgow, G3 8DP
Tel: 0141 357 3929
Small collection of motorcycles includes Automobile
Association BSA combination. Open Monday to Saturday
10am-5pm. Sunday 11am-5pm. Closed December 25 and
January 1. Admission free.

Myreton Motor Museum
Aberlady, Longniddry, East Lothian, EH32 0PZ
Tel: 018757 288
Small collection of motorcycles includes 1926 350cc
Chater-Lea racer and Egli Vincent. Open Easter to October
10am-5pm and October to Easter 10am-6pm. Closed
December 25 and January 1. Adults £2, children 50p.

National Motor Museum
Brockenhurst, Beaulieu, SO42 7ZN
Tel: 01590 612123/612345
Important motorcycle collection. Reference and
photographic libraries. Open Easter to September 10am-
6pm, October to Easter 10am-5pm. Closed December 25.
Adults £6.75, OAPs/students £5.25, children £4.75
(includes Museum, rides and drives, Monastic Life
Exhibition and entry to Palace House and grounds).

National Motorcycle Museum
Coventry Road, Bickenhill, Solihull, B92 0EJ.
Tel: 01675 53311

Royal Museum of Scotland
Chambers Street, Edinburgh, EH1 1JF
Tel: 0131 225 7534
Small display of engines and complete machines includes
the world's first 4 cylinder motorcycle, an 1895 Holden.
Open Monday to Saturday 10am-5pm. Sunday 2pm-5pm.
Closed December 25, January 1. Admission free.

Science Museum
Exhibition Road, South Kensington, SW7 2DD
Tel: 0171 589 3456
Interesting collection of engines and complete machines,
including cutaway BSA A10 and Yamaha XS1100. Recent
additions to displays include 1940 500cc BMW and 1969
Honda CB750. Open Monday to Saturday 10am-6pm.
Sunday 11am-6pm. Closed December 24-26. Adults £4,
OAPs and children £2.10, disabled free. The bulk of the
Science Museum's motorcycle collection is stored at
Wroughton Airfield near Swindon, Wilts.
Tel: 0793 814466.

Stanford Hall Motorcycle Museum
Stanford Hall, Lutterworth, LE17 6DH
Tel: 01788 860250
A collection of older machines and racers. Open Saturdays,
Sundays, Bank Holiday Mondays and following Tuesdays
Easter to September, 2.30pm-6pm. (12 noon-6pm when a
special event is taking place.). Admission to grounds:
Adults £1.60, children 70p. Motorcycle Museum: Adults
90p, children 20p.

DIRECTORY OF MOTORCYCLE CLUBS

If you would like your Club to be included in next year's directory or if you have a change of address or telephone number, please inform us by 30th April 1998. Entries will be repeated in susequent editions unless we are requested otherwise.

ABC Owners Club, D A Hales, The Hedgerows, Sutton St Nicholas, Hereford HR1 3BU Tel: 01432 880726
Aermacchi Harley-Davidson Motor Club, Tuninfluiter 74, 3906, NS Veenendaal, The Netherlands.
Aircooled RD Club, Susan Gregory (Membership Secretary), 6 Baldwin Road, Burnage, Greater Manchester M19 1LY Tel: 0161 286 7539
AJS & Matchless Owners Club, Northants Classic Bike Centre, 25 Victoria Street, Irthlingborough, Northamptonshire NN9 5RG Tel: 01933 652155
AMC Owners Club, c/o Terry Corley, 12 Chilworth Gardens, Sutton, Surrey SM1 3SP
Androd Classics, 70 Broadway, Frome, Somerset BA11 3HE Tel: 01373 471087
Ariel Owners Club, Andy Hemingway, 80 Pasture Lane, Clayton, Bradford, Yorkshire BD14 6LN Tel: 01274 882141
Ariel Owners Motor Cycle Club, Swindon Branch, 45 Wheeler Avenue, Swindon, Wiltshire SN2 6HQ
BMW Club, c/o John Lawes (Vintage Secretary), Bowbury House, Kirk Langley, Ashbourne, Derbyshire DE6 4NJ Tel: 01332 824334
Bantam Enthusiasts Club, c/o Vic Salmon, 16 Oakhurst Close, Walderslade, Chatham, Kent ME5 9AN
Benelli Motobi Riders Club, c/o Stephen Peace, 43 Sherrington Road, Ipswich, Suffolk IP1 4HT
Benelli Owners Club, c/o Rosie Marston, 14 Rufford Close, Barton Seagrave, Kettering, Northamptonshire NN15 6RF
Benelli/Motobi Owners Group, Stuart Ellinson, 68 Lapage Street, Bradford, Yorkshire BD3 8EH
Best Feet Forward MCC, Ian Leslie, 14 Haredale Road, London SE24 0AF Tel: 0171 274 7526
BMW Owners Club, c/o Mike Cox, 22 Combermere, Thornbury, Bristol, Avon BS12 2ET Tel: 01454 415358
Bristol & Avon Roadrunners Motorcycle Club, 177 Speedwell Road, Speedwell, Bristol, Avon BS5 7SP
Bristol & District Sidecar Club, 158 Fairlyn Drive, Kingswood, Bristol, Avon BS15 4PZ
Bristol Genesis Motorcycle Club, Burrington, 1a Bampton Close, Headley Park, Bristol, Avon BS13 7QZ Tel: 0117 978 2584
British Motor Bike Owners Club, c/o Ray Peacock, Crown Inn, Shelfanger, Diss, Norfolk IP22 2DL
British Motorcycle Owners Club, c/o Phil Coventry, 59 Mackenzie Street, Bolton, Lancashire BL1 6QP
British Motorcyclists Federation, Jack Wiley House, 129 Seaforth Avenue, Motspur Park, New Malden, Surrey KT3 6JU
British Two-Stroke Club, Ralph Hynn (Membership Secretary), 32 Glebe Gardens, Harlington, Bedfordshire LU6 5PE
Brough Superior Club, c/o Piers Otley, 6 Canning Road, Felpham, Sussex PO22 7AD
BSA Owners Club, Rob Jones, 44 Froxfield Road, West Leigh, Havant, Hampshire PO9 5PW
CBX Riders Club, c/o Peter Broad, 57 Osborne Close, Basingstoke, Hampshire RG21 2TS
Chiltern Vehicle Preservation Group, Chiltern House, Aylesbury, Buckinghamshire HP17 8BY Tel: 01296 651283
Christian Motorcyclists Association, PO Box 113, Wokingham, Berkshire RG11 5UB
Classic Kawasaki Club (Formerly The Kawasaki Triples Club), PO Box 235, Nottingham, Nottinghamshire NG8 6DT
Classic Racing Motorcycle Club Ltd, Peter Haylock Membership Secretary, 19 Kenilworth Avenue, Harold Farm, Romford, Essex RM3 9ME
Cossack Owners Club, Phil Hardcastle, 19 Elms Road, Bare, Morecambe, Lancashire LA4 6AP
Cotton Owners & Enthusiasts Club, Stan White, 62 Cook Street, Avonmouth, Bristol, Dorset BS11
Dot Owners Club, c/o Chris Black, 115 Lincoln Avenue, Clayton, Newcastle-upon-Tyne, Tyne & Wear ST5 3AR
Ducati Owners Club, Martin Littlebury 32 Lawrence Moorings, Sawbridgeworth, Hertfordshire CM21 9PE
Federation of Sidecars, Barry Miller Membership Secretary, 1 Bartin Cottage, Sutton Cullompton, EX15 1NF Tel: 01884 34533
Fellowship of Christian Motorcyclists, Janice Thomson, The Treehouse, 22 Charlotte Gardens, Collier Row, Romford, Essex RM5 2ED

FJ Owners Club, Karen Everett (Membership Secretary), 13 Severn Close, Charfield, Wotton-U-Edge, Gloucestershire GL12 8TZ Tel: 01454 261737
Forgotten Racing Club, Mrs Chris Pinches, 73 High Street, Morton, Bourne, Lincolnshire PE10 0NR Tel: 01778 570535
Francis Barnett Owners Club, 58 Knowle Road, Totterdown, Bristol, Avon BS4 2ED
Gilera Network, Pete Fisher, 4 Orton Grove, Penn, Wolverhampton WV4 4JN Tel: 01902 337626
Gold Star Owners Club, c/o George Chiswell, 43 Church Lane, Kitts Green, Birmingham, West Midlands B33 9EG
Goldwing Owners Club, 82 Farley Close, Little Stoke, Bristol, Avon BS12 6HG
Greeves Riders Association, Dave & Brenda McGregor, 4 Longshaw Close, North Wingfield, Chesterfield, Staffordshire S42 5QR Tel: 01246 853846
Harley Davidson Manufacturers Club. Tel: 01280 700101
Harley Davidson Owners Club, 1 St Johns Road, Clifton, Bristol, Avon BS8 2ET
Harley Davidson Riders Club of Great Britain, SAE to Membership Secretary, PO Box 62, Newton Abbott, Devon TQ12 2QE
Harley Owners Group, HOG UK, The Bell Tower, High Street, Brackley, Northamptonshire NN13 7DT Tel: 01280 700101
Hedingham Sidecar Owners Club, John Dean (Membership Secretary), Hollington Fields Cottage, Fole Lane, Stoke-on-Trent Tel: 01889 507389
Hesketh Owners Club, Peter Whitc, 1 Nurthfield Road, Soham, Cambridgeshire CB7 5UE
Historic Raleigh Motorcycle Club, c/o R. Thomas, 22 Valley Road, Solihull, West Midlands B92 9AD
Honda Owners Club (GB), Membership Secretary, 61 Vicarage Road, Ware, Hertfordshire SG12 7BE Tel: 01932 787111
Indian Motorcycle Club, c/o John Chatterton (Membership Secretary), 183 Buxton Road, Newtown, Disley, Stockport, Stockport, Cheshire SK12 3RA Tel: 01663 747106 (after 6pm)
International CBX Owners Association, 24 Pevensey Way, Paddock Hill, Frimley, Camberley, Surrey GU16 5YJ Tel: 01252 836698
International Laverda Owners Club, c/o Alan Cudipp, 29 Claypath Road, Hetton-le-Hole, Houghton-le-Spring, Tyne & Wear DH5 0EL
International Motorcyclists Tour Club, James Clegg, 238 Methane Road, Netherton, Huddersfield, Yorkshire HD4 7HL Tel: 01484 664868
Italian Motorcycle Owners Club, John Riches (Membership Secretary), 12 Wappenham Road, Abthorpe, Towcester, Northamptonshire NN12 8QU
Jawa-CZ Owners Club, John Blackburn 39 Bignor Road, Sheffield, Yorkshire S6 1JD
Kawasaki GT Club, D. Shucksmith, Club Secretary, Flat K, Lichfield Court, Lichfield Road, Walsall, West Midlands WS4 2DX Tel: 01922 37441
Kawasaki Owners Club, c/o John Dalton, 37 Hinton Road, Runcorn, Cheshire WA7 5PZ
Kawasaki Riders Club, Gemma, Court 1, Concord House, Kirmington, Humberside DN39 6YP
L E Velo Club Ltd, Kevin Parsons, Chapel Mead, Blandford Hill, Winterbourne, Whitechurch, Blandford, Dorset DT11 0AB
Laverda Owners Club, c/o Ray Sheepwash, 8 Maple Close, Swanley, Kent BR8 7YN
LE Velo Owners Club, P. Walker, Grantley House, Warwicks Bench, Guildford, Surrey GU1 3SZ
London Douglas Motorcycle Club, c/o Reg Holmes (Membership Secretary), 48 Standish Avenue, Stoke Lodge, Patchway, Bristol, Avon BS12 6AG
Maico Owners Club, c/o Phil Hingston, 'No Elms', Goosey, Faringdon, Oxfordshire SN7 8PA Tel: 01367 710408
Marston Sunbeam Register, IMI Marston Ltd, Wobaston Road, Fordhouses, Wolverhampton, West Midlands WV10 6QJ
Military Vehicle Trust, PO Box 6, Fleet, Hampshire GU13 9PE
Morgan Three-Wheeler Club Ltd, Dennis Plater Holbrooks, Thoby Lane, Mountnessing, Brentwood, Essex CM15 0TA Tel: 01277 352867

Morini Owners Club, c/o Richard Laughton, 20 Fairford Close, Church Hill, Redditch, Hereford & Worcester B98 9LU

Morini Riders Club, c/o Kevin Bennett, 1 Glebe Farm Cottages, Sutton Veney, Warminster, Wiltshire BA12 7AS

Moto Guzzi Club GB, Andy Harris (Membership Secretary), 158 Vale Road, Windsor, Berkshire SL4 5JN

Motorcycle Action Group, PO Box 750, Kings Norton, Birmingham, West Midlands B30 3BA

MV Agusta Club GB, c/o Martyn Simpkins, 31 Baker Street, Stapenhill, Burton-on-Trent, Staffordshire DE15 9AF

MV Agusta Owners Club, A. Elderton, 108 Thundersley Park Road, South Benfleet, Staffordshire SS7 1ES

National Association for Bikers with a Disability (NABD), Rick Hulse, 39 Lownorth Road, Wythenshaw, Greater Manchester M22 0JU

National Autocycle & Cyclemotor Club, 92 Waveney Road, Ipswich, Suffolk IP1 5DG

National Hill Climb Association, 43 Tyler Close, Hanham, Bristol, Avon BS15 3RG Tel: 0117 944 3569

National Scooter Riders Association, PO Box 32, Mansfield, Nottinghamshire NG19

National Sprint Association, 84 Fairholme Crescent, Hayes, Middlesex UB4 8QT

National Trailers Owners Club (NaTo), 47c Uplands Avenue, Rowley, Regis Warley, West Midlands B65 9PU

New Imperial Owners Association, c/o Mike Slater, 3 Fairview Drive, Higham, Kent ME3 7BG

North Devon British Motorcycle Owners Club, 47 Old Town, Bideford, Devon EX39 3BH Tel: 01237 472237

Norton Owners Club, c/o Dave Fenner, Beeches, Durley Brook Road, Durley, Southhampton, Hampshire SO32 2AR

Norton Owners Club, Cambridge Branch, William Riches (Secretary), 8 Coombelands Road, Royston, Hertfordshire SG8 7DW Tel: 01763 245131

Norton Rotary Enthusiasts Club, Alan Jones, 112 Fairfield Crescent, Newhall, Swadlingcote, Derbyshire DE11 0TB

Panther Owners Club, Graham & Julie Dibbins, Oakdene, 22 Oak Street, Netherton, West Midlands DY2 9LJ

Professional and Executive Motorcyclists' Club, Paul Morris, Stonecroft, 43 Finedon Road, Irthlingborough, Northamptonshire NN9 5TY

Riders for Health, The Old Vicarage, Norton, Daventry, Northamptonshire NN11 5ND Tel: 01327 300047

Rotary Owners' Club, c/o David Cameron, Dunbar, Ingatestone Road, Highwood, Chelmsford, Essex CM1 3QU

Royal Enfield Owners Club, c/o John Cherry (Secretary), Diments Cottage, 50 Dorchester Road, Stratton, Dorchester, Avon DT2 9RZ

Rudge Enthusiasts Club Ltd, c/o Colin Kirkwood, 41 Rectory Green, Beckenham, Kent BR3 4HX Tel: 0181 658 0494

Scott Owners Club, Brian Marshall, Walnut Cottage, Abbey Lane, Aslockton, Nottingham, Nottinghamshire NG13 9AE Tel: 01949 851027

Shrivenham Motorcycle Club, 12-14 Townsend Road, Shrivenham, Swindon, Wiltshire SN6 8AS

Sidecar Register, c/o John Proctor, 112 Briarlyn Road, Birchencliffe, Huddersfield, Yorkshire HD3 3NW

Street Specials Motorcycle Club inc Rickman O/C, Harris O/C & Featherbed O/C, c/o Dominic Dawson, 12 St Mark's Close, Gosport, Hampshire PO12 2DB Tel: 01705 501321

Sunbeam MCC, Peter Donaldson, 28 Lesney Park Road, Erith, Kent DA8 3DG

Sunbeam Owners Club, David Jordan (Membership Secretary), 72 Chart Lane, Reigate, Surrey RH2 7EA

Sunbeam Owners Club, Stewart Engineering, Church Terrace, Harbury, Leamington Spa, Warwickshire CV33 9HL

Sunbeam Owners Fellowship, PO Box 7, Market Harborough, Leicestershire LE16

Surrey Vintage Scooter Club, 8 Amesbury Close, Worcester Park, Surrey KT4 8PW Tel: 0181 337 2534

Suzuki Kettle Club, Fred Dear, 104 Ranley Road, Locksheath, Southampton, Hampshire SO31 6PD

Suzuki Owners Club, Mark Fitz-Gibbon (Membership Secretary), 3 Rossetti Lodge, Burns Road, Royston, Hertfordshire SG8 5SF

Tamworth & District Classic Motorcycle Club. Tel: Tamworth 281244

The Vmax Club, 87 Honiton Road, Wyken, Coventry, Warwickshire CV2 3EF Tel: 01203 442054

Trail Riders Fellowship, Tony Stuart, 'Cambrea', Trebetherick, Wadebridge, Cornwall PL27 6SG Tel: 01208 862960

Trident and Rocket 3 Owners Club, PO Box 159, Cobham , Surrey KT11 2YG

Triumph Motorcycle Club, 6 Hortham Lane, Almondsbury, Bristol, Avon BS12 4JH

Triumph Owners Club, c/o Mrs M Mellish, 4 Douglas Avenue, Harold Wood, Romford, Essex RM3 0UT

Triumph Triples Club, H. J. Allen, 50 Sylmond Gardens, Rushden , Northamptonshire NN10 9EJ

Velocette Owners Club, Stuart Smith, 18 Hazel Road, Rubery, Birmingham, West Midlands B45 9DX

Velocette Owners Club, Vic Blackman (Secretary), 1 Mayfair, Tilehurst, Reading, Berkshire RG3 4RA

Veteran Grass Track Riders Association (VGTRA). Tel: 01622 204745

Vincent HRD Owners Club, c/o John Wilding (Information Officer), Little Wildings, Fairhazel, Piltdown, Uckfield, Sussex TN22 3XB Tel: 01825 763529

Vincent Owners Club, Andy Davenport, Ashley Cottage, 133 Bath Road, Atworth, Wiltshire SN12 8LB

Vintage Japanese Motorcycle Club, PO Box 515, Dartford, Kent DA1 3RE

Vintage Motor Cycle Club, Allen House, Wetmore Road, Burton-on-Trent, Staffordshire DE14 1TR Tel: 01283 540557

Vintage Motor Cycle Club (Peterborough Branch), Jeremy Boycott Thurston (Secretary), 34 Heath Road, Helpston, Peterborough, Cambridgeshire PE6 7EG

Vintage Motor Scooter Club, c/o Ian Harrop, 11 Ivanhoe Avenue, Lowton St Lukes, Nr Warrington, Cheshire WA3 2HX

Vintage Motorcycle Club of Ulster, c/o Mrs M Burns, 20 Coach Road, Comber, Newtownards, Co Down, Ireland BT23 5QX

Virago Owners Club, John Bryning, River Green House, Great Sampford, Saffron Walden, Essex CB10 2RS Tel: 01799 586578

Womans International Motorcycle Association, PO Box 612, Bristol, Avon BS99 5UQ

Yamaha Riders Club, Alan Cheney, 11 Lodden Road, Farnborough, Hampshire GU14 9NR

ZI Owners Club, c/o Sam Holt, 54 Hawthorne Close, Congleton, Cheshire CW12 4UF

Italic numbers denote colour pages

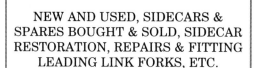

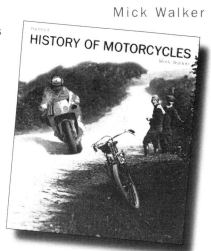